D0889148

Terran

The Quirky Tourist Guide to the Great Smoky Mountains National Park
(including Gatlinburg, Sevierville, Pigeon Forge, Bryson City & Cherokee)

Terrance Zepke

The Quirky Tourist Guide to The Great Smoky Mountains National Park | Terrance Zepke

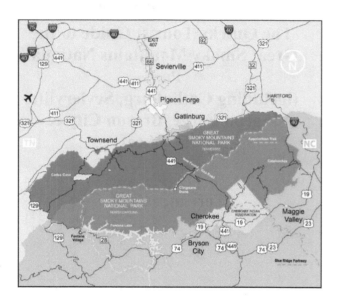

Copyright © 2023 by Terrance Zepke

All queries should be directed to: www.safaripublishing.net.

For more about the author: www.terrancezepke.com and www.terrancetalkstravel.com

Zepke, Terrance

Terrance Talks Travel: The Quirky Tourist Guide to the Great Smoky Mountains National Park

1. Travel-Tennessee Mountains.
2. Travel-North Carolina Mountains.
3. The Smokies. 4. Gatlinburg.
5. Sevierville. 6. Pigeon Forge.
7. Cherokee. 8. Cades Cove. 9. Family Travel. 10. National Parks-Hiking & Wildlife. 11. Great Smoky Mountains National Park Adventures & Daytrips. 12. Dining & Lodging in The Smokies. I. Title.

ISBN: 9781942738824

Safari Publishing

CONTENTS

The Quirky Tourist Guide to The Great Smoky Mountains National Park | Terrance Zepke

INTRODUCTION

I have to admit that I thought this book would be one of my easier projects. After all, my family had a home in the Smokies for years. My best friend lived in Townsend (just outside the park). I grew up wandering the streets of Gatlinburg, going tubing, swimming in The Sinks (when you could still do that), driving the Cades Cove Loop during fall colors (now known as leaf peeping) every year, enjoying weekend hikes and picnics, and exploring all over the park. Also, I got one of my degrees from the University of Tennessee. My friends and I spent many weekends up in the mountains (when the Vols weren't playing). And I still go a couple of times a year to use my

annual Dollywood pass. I love the
Christmas shows!

So this book project was going to be
easy peasy, right? *Wrong!* When I
started my research, I realized there's
a lot I knew, but there was a lot more
I didn't know.

I discovered all kinds of great trails
and scenic loops. I didn't know much
about the other entrances and gateway
cities since I always enter via
Gatlinburg. Also, I didn't realize there
was so many historic buildings and
waterfalls—or wildlife. I don't know
where those wild turkeys and boars
are hiding, but I've never seen them!

I leaned about a few hidden gems that
I wish I'd known about sooner. I also
found out some resources and tips I

certainly wish I'd known about before
now.

Now what I did know is that this is a
great place for all kinds of people,
from honeymooners to families. There
are so many things to see and do that
there is something for everyone. And
so much is FREE! It's one of the most
affordable vacations you can take
(depending on optional attractions).

This includes admission to the Great
Smoky Mountains National Park.
There is no entrance fee like most
parks charge. You can come back
every day for a week and pay nothing.
Zero. Zilch. Nada. Most parks charge
$10 -$20pp or $25 - $35 per
motorcycle or vehicle *daily*.

Great Smoky Mountains National Park is within a day's drive of two-thirds of the nation's population.

The flora and fauna and wildlife are among some of the most diverse of our nation's parks. There are hundreds of bird species, plus mammals, amphibians, reptiles, and fish. There are thirty species of salamanders alone! Every May, Mother Nature throws a spectacular firefly show. It is so popular there is a lottery for tickets. Beautiful wildflowers grow all over the place. There is even a Spring Wildflower Pilgrimage!

Did you know that the Great Smoky Mountains National Park is within a day's drive of two-thirds of this country's population?

I'm sure these are all reasons
contributing to the park's popularity.
Did you know the Great Smoky
Mountains National Park is the most
visited park in America? It is #1! Not
even Yellowstone, Zion, Grand
Tetons, or the Grand Canyon National
Parks come close. There have been
more than 500,000,000 visitors since
1934. That's 500 million people that
have come through the park since it
was established. The park averages 13
million visitors annually.

Whoa! That's a lot of people! The
point of this reference is to share
everything great about this park and
its gateway communities AND to
show you how to best enjoy it. I will
share tips and lesser known routes so
that you don't spend your vacation

sitting in traffic or searching for
parking.

Planning is everything with a national
park vacation. It is especially
important if you are traveling with
small children or anyone with special
needs. Advance reservations, tickets,
and a game plan are a must! I share
what you need to know so you can go
and have a (hassle-free) great time.

Furthermore, I want to reveal unique
ways you can experience this special
place. There are some super cool and
totally unusual lodging choices to be
considered, as well as some little-
known activities (be sure to read
Terrance's Top Ten Picks chapter).

So read on to discover the two best
day drives in The Smokies, four

favorite motorcycle routes, two places in the park you must visit, five best things to see in Cades Cove, best trails for strollers and doggies, and much more!

GETTING THERE

<u>By Air</u>

The closest major airport on the Tennessee side to the Great Smoky Mountains National Park is **McGee-Tyson Airport** in Alcoa, Tennessee, twelve miles from downtown Knoxville. It's a 40-mile drive from the airport to the Gatlinburg park entrance. The airport is served by several commercial airlines. All major

rental car agencies are at this airport.
www.flyknoxville.com

On the North Carolina side, **Asheville Regional Airport** is the closest commercial airport in Fletcher, North Carolina, fourteen miles south of downtown Asheville. It's a 41-mile drive from the airport to the Cherokee park entrance. The airport is served by several commercial airlines. All major rental car companies are at this airport. www.flyavl.com

By Land

There are three main entrances into The Great Smoky Mountains National Park:

Gatlinburg, TN entrance is the most popular point of entry. From I-40 take Exit 407 (Sevierville) to TN-66 South. At the main intersection in Sevierville, continue straight onto US-441 South. Follow

US-441 through Sevierville and
Pigeon Forge into park.

From Sevierville and Pigeon Forge:
Stay straight on US-441 South and
continue into the park.

Townsend, TN entrance
From the north: From I-40 in
Knoxville take Exit 386B to US-129
South to Alcoa/Maryville. At
Maryville proceed on US-321
North/TN -73 East through
Townsend. Continue straight on TN-
73 into the park.

From the south: From I-75 take Exit
376 to I-140 E towards Oak
Ridge/Maryville. Merge onto I-140 E
via Exit 376B towards Maryville.
Turn onto US-129 South (Alcoa
Highway) at Exit 11A and travel
towards Alcoa. Turn onto TN-35 and
follow it to US-321 North. Follow
US-321 North/TN -73 East through

Townsend. Continue straight on TN-73 into the park.

From Pigeon Forge: Turn at red light #3 and take US-321 south into Townsend. Then take 73 East into the National Park.

Cherokee, NC entrance

From the north: From I-40, take Exit 27 to US-74 West towards Waynesville. Turn onto US-19 and proceed through Maggie Valley to Cherokee. Turn onto US-441 North at Cherokee and follow the road into the park.

From the south: Follow US-441/US-23 North. At Dillsboro merge on US-74 West/US-441 North. At Exit 74 merge onto US-441. Follow US-441 through Cherokee and into the park.

IMPORTANT UPDATE!

 **FYI: Parking passes are now required for the park. See "Getting Around" later in this chapter for more information.**

Distance from Gatlinburg (closest city to the park) to...
Charlotte, NC=196 miles
Atlanta, GA=256 miles
Raleigh, NC=325 miles
Charleston, SC=338 miles
Columbus, OH=400 miles
Pittsburgh, PA=496 miles
Jacksonville, FL=512 miles
Baton Rouge, LA=699 miles
New York City, NY=720 miles
Miami, FL=858 miles

The best way to get around Great Smoky Mountains National Park is by car. The park does not offer any guided tours and there is no public transportation to the park.

More Options

Amtrak offers 7-day vacation packages to the park. There is no direct Amtrak service to the park or nearby cities at this time. https://www.amtrakvacations.com/destinations/great-smoky-mountains-national-park-tn

Greyhound Lines does not offer service to the park area at this time. www.greyhound.com

Tourist Towns & Cities close to the Great Smoky Mountains National Park
- Gatlinburg, TN. 7.6 miles
- Pigeon Forge, TN. 14.4 miles
- Sevierville, TN. 21 miles
- Townsend, TN. 24.5 miles
- Cherokee, NC. 27.9 miles
- Bryson City, NC. 38.1 miles

Getting Around the Great Smoky Mountains NP

The Great Smoky Mountains extends through the following cities:

- Pigeon Forge, TN
- Gatlinburg, TN
- Sevierville, TN
- Townsend, TN
- Cosby, TN
- Wears Valley, TN
- Cherokee, NC
- Bryson City, NC
- Elkmont, TN
- Maryville, TN

Shuttle Service

Parking at Laurel Falls, Clingmans Dome and other popular locations within the Great Smoky Mountains National Park can fill up quickly.

Local shuttle services can help visitors access many park destinations where parking is very limited. The shuttles will pick up and drop off at Alum Cave Trail, Laurel Falls Trail, Chimney Tops Trail, Trillium Gap Trail (Grotto Falls), Rainbow Falls Trail, and Clingmans Dome. There are six companies offering shuttle services.

- AAA Hiker Shuttle, www.aaahikerservice.com
- A Walk in the Woods, www.awalkinthewoods.com
- Bryson City Outdoors, www.brysoncityoutdoors.com
- Great Smoky Mountains Eco Tours, https://greatsmokymountaineco tours.com/shuttle-services/
- RockyTop Tours, www.rockytoptours.com

- **Smoky Mountain Rides,** www.smokyrides.com

Rideshare: Uber and **Lyft** are available in most towns and cities surrounding the park but not in the park itself.

There are taxis and car services that service area towns and cities, such as **Angels Taxi Service,** https://angelstaxiservice.com/ and **Smoky Mountain Taxi,** www.smokymtntaxi.com

FYI: The Waze travel app provides real time traffic updates and notifies users of area accidents and roadwork, as well as ETA.
https://www.waze.com

Follow @SmokiesRoadsNPS on Twitter for the most up to date road closures and other important information.

Visitor Welcome Centers
Four visitor centers are located within the national park at **Sugarlands** (1420 Fighting Creek Gap Road, Gatlinburg, TN), **Oconaluftee** (1194 Newfound Gap Rd, Cherokee, NC), **Cades Cove** (5686 Cades Cove Loop Rd, Townsend, TN), and **Clingmans Dome** (Clingmans Dome Rd, Bryson City, NC).

Also, there is the **Gatlinburg Welcome Center**, 1011 Banner Rd., Gatlinburg, TN) and **Great Smoky Mountains Association Visitor Center and Store** (2 Everett St, Bryson City, NC).

FYI: In the pioneer days, mountain apples were used in many recipes, such as dried apple shortcake, apple fritters, apple butter, apple cobbler, applesauce, apple pie and pan-fried apples.

Great Smoky Mountains National Park

WHAT YOU NEED TO
KNOW...*Read carefully!*

<u>Cost</u>
One of the main reasons the Great
Smoky Mountains National Park is so
popular is because it's one of the only
national parks in the United States
that does NOT charge an entrance fee.
That's right! ***No admission fee!***

Parking

Even though park admission is FREE, parking is not. Parking tags are required for all vehicles parked for more than 15 minutes starting March 1, 2023. Tags will be available for all vehicle sizes and types:

- Daily - $5
- Weekly - $15
- Annual - $40

'PARK IT FORWARD' PARKING PROGRAM BEGAN ON MARCH 1, 2023. There are no exemptions or exceptions. Passes can be purchased on site at all visitor's center or online in advance at **https://www.smokymountainnaviga tor.com/parking-passes/ www.recreation.gov**

Best Time to Visit

The Great Smoky Mountains National Park is *THE MOST VISITED NATIONAL PARK IN THE COUNTRY*, averaging 12 million visitors annually (14.1 in 2021 according to the NPS).

FYI: The Great Smoky Mountains National Park gets three times the annual visitors that runner-up Yellowstone National Park receives!

The busiest months to visit Great Smoky Mountains are **June, July, August and October** (for the fall colors), with one million visitors entering the park during each month. The park offers miles of wooded trails, stunning waterfalls, winding scenic drives, close to 100 historic structures and lots of educational exhibits. Winter and spring are also good times to visit with less crowds and traffic. Just be mindful there may be some road closures in the park due to weather conditions.

Weather

Elevations in the Smokies range significantly, from 875 feet to 6,643 feet. Temperatures can vary 10-20∘F from mountain base to the top. Also, clear skies at the base do not

guarantee good weather at higher
elevations. Rainfall averages 55
inches per year in the lowlands to 85
inches per year at Clingmans Dome,
the highest point in the park. Plan
accordingly with the right clothes and
gear.

Hours

24/7. Yep, that's right. The park is
open all the time, year-round. So
come early to avoid crowds and
traffic. Or come late to avoid them. It
stays light until 9 or 10 during peak
summer months. Primary roads are
always open (weather permitting) and
secondary roads are open seasonally.

 **FYI: Cell phone service is unavailable in many park locations, including Cades Cove and in Cataloochee. It is usually available in the surrounding communities.**

Directions

Great Smoky Mountains National Park straddles the borders of the states of Tennessee and North Carolina. The three main entrances to the park are in Gatlinburg, TN; Townsend, TN; and Cherokee, NC.

Gatlinburg, TN entrance
From I-40 take Exit 407 (Sevierville) to TN-66 South. At the Sevierville intersection, continue straight onto US-441 South. Follow US-441

through Sevierville and Pigeon Forge
into park.

Townsend, TN entrance
From the north: From I-40 in
Knoxville take Exit 386B to US-129
South to Alcoa/Maryville. At
Maryville proceed on US-321
North/TN -73 East through
Townsend. Continue straight on TN-
73 into the park.

From the south: From interstate
highway I-75 take Exit 376 to I-140 E
towards Oak Ridge/Maryville. Merge
onto I-140 E via Exit 376B towards
Maryville. Turn onto US-129 South
(Alcoa Highway) at Exit 11A and
travel towards Alcoa. Turn onto TN-
35 and follow it to US-321 North.
Follow US-321 North/TN -73 East

through Townsend. Continue straight
on TN-73 into the park.

Cherokee, NC entrance
From the north: From I-40, take Exit
27 to US-74 West towards
Waynesville. Turn onto US-19 and
proceed through Maggie Valley to
Cherokee. Turn onto US-441 North at
Cherokee and follow the road into the
park.

From the south: Follow US-441/US-
23 North. At Dillsboro merge on US-
74 West/US-441 North. At Exit 74
merge onto US-441. Follow US-441
through Cherokee and into the park.

FYI: Do not trust your vehicle's GPS because it may provide incorrect driving directions in the mountains, such as sending you down one-way roads the wrong way or down dead-end roads. Free park road maps are available in all visitor centers and they can also be downloaded at https://www.nps.gov/grsm/planyour visit/maps.htm

Tennessee vs. North Carolina

Should I visit the Tennessee side or
the North Carolina side of Smokies?
Which is best?

No worries. *"It's all good!"* There is
no bad side of the park, it just depends
on what you're looking for.

The Tennessee side is known as the
adventure side while the North
Carolina side is known as the tranquil
side. More people enter through the
Tennessee side.

But as to which is best, it depends on
what you're looking for. North
Carolina has elk, which were re-
introduced to the Cataloochee
Valley and haven't yet spread over to
the Tennessee side of the park.

Otherwise, wildlife is very similar. Black bears are seen on both the North Carolina and Tennessee sides of the national park. There are around 1,700 bears in the park, which is around two bears per square mile for either side.

Peak visitation months differ for the two sides. July is the highest visitation month for the Tennessee side, while October is most popular on the North Carolina side. That's because more people go to that side to see the fall colors even though they are brilliant from both sides.

The Tennessee side of the national park is famous for its many attractions and tourist towns located right outside of the park, including Pigeon Forge and Gatlinburg.

While Tennessee may have more
attractions (and more dining,
shopping, and lodging options)
directly outside of the park's
boundaries, both states have unique
appeals inside of the Smokies.

The North Carolina side is not as
heavily visited so you will enjoy
quieter hikes with great scenery at
Deep Creek and Cataloochee Valley
and you will have an easier time
motoring around due to less traffic.
Cherokee has a lot of cultural
activities and Bryson City is a nice
walking town.

Pets

Dogs are allowed in campgrounds,
picnic areas, and along the roads, but
must be kept on a leash at all times.
The leash must not exceed 6 feet in

length. Two short walking paths permit dogs—the **Gatlinburg Trail** and the **Oconaluftee River Trail**. Pets are not allowed on any other park trails.

Camping
The park offers different types of campsites:

Backcountry - for backpackers. Requires hiking several miles to a site located in the park's backcountry. Reservations and permits are required. https://smokiespermits.nps.gov/

Frontcountry - camping near your car in a developed campground that has restrooms with cold running water and flush toilets. Each campsite has a fire grate and picnic table. https://www.nps.gov/grsm/planyourvi

sit/frontcountry-camping.htm

Group Campgrounds - large campsites (in frontcountry campgrounds) suitable for groups of eight or more.
https://www.nps.gov/grsm/planyourvi sit/groupcamps.htm

Horse Camps - small campgrounds, that offer hitch racks for horses and primitive camping facilities.
https://www.nps.gov/grsm/planyourvi sit/horsecamps.htm

There are lots of RV parks and campgrounds (with log cabin rentals) in the nearby communities to the park—we're talking 100+! No matter where you want to stay, there will be campgrounds to choose from.
https://campgrounds.rvlife.com/region

s/tennessee/great-smoky-mountains-
national-park

Best Scenic Drives & Overlooks

Foothills Parkway was authorized by
Congress in 1944 but only 22.5 miles
of the 72-mile corridor have been
completed. The parkway is the oldest
unfinished highway project in
Tennessee. Challenging terrain and
funding issues are the main reasons
the parkway is still incomplete. It is
predicted that it will be at least twenty
years before it is finished.
However, the National Park Service
recently announced the final phase of
construction on the 16-mile stretch of
the Foothills Parkway between
Walland, TN and Wears Valley, TN.
Now that this section of the Parkway
is paved, motorists will be able to

enjoy a scenic 33-mile drive from
Chilhowee Lake to Sevier County.

Good news! The "missing link"
connecting Wears Valley to Lake
Chilhowee will soon be completed,
adding 15.8 miles to the parkway.
Motorists will enjoy views of the
Townsend Valley as they traverse this
stretch of road.

Foothills Parkway (Exit 443 off I-
40) is an alternate route to Hwy 321
from Pigeon Forge to Townsend. You
can access the roadway from Wears
Valley, Townsend, and on west to
Walland. Many people visiting the
area come in from the north, and
Walland is the most used access point.
RVs and trailers are allowed on the
parkway.

Caylor Gap Overlook offers the best view of any scenic overlook on the Foothills Parkway. A large parking area on one side of the road has plenty of room for vehicles and a pull-off on the opposite side has room for campers and RVs.

FYI: Although maintained by the NPS, Foothills Parkway is not technically inside the park. Be careful about speeding on the parkway because speed limits are strictly enforced.

Newfound Gap Road (US-441) is considered to be one of the most scenic park drives. Beginning elevation is 1,289 feet but the road climbs to 5,046 feet at Newfound Gap, which is the lowest drivable pass in the park. From Newfound Gap, the elevation descends to 1,991 feet at Cherokee, NC. Best overlooks: Campbell Overlook, Chimney Tops Overlook, Morton Overlook, and Oconoluftee Valley Overlook (watch for signs).

FYI: Newfound Gap is where President Roosevelt formally dedicated the park in 1940. It also marks the TN/NC state line.

Little River Road is twenty-five miles long and is actually comprised of three roads: Little River Gorge

Road, Laurel Creek Road, and
Fighting Creek Gap Road. This road
connects Sugarlands Visitor Center
(near Gatlinburg) to Cades Cove.
During this low elevation drive, you
will pass through some lovely areas of
the park, including Elkmont Ghost
Town, Sinks Waterfall, and
Townsend Wye swimming hole.
Many consider this one of the best
routes through the Smokies.

Roaring Fork Motor Trail is another
popular driving route because it
begins and ends in Gatlinburg. This is
a one-way road that is accessed at red
light #8 in Gatlinburg. This low-
elevation route includes Ogle
Farmstead and "the place of 1,000
drips, a roadside waterfall. Only
vehicles are permitted on this road (no
campers, RVs, buses, or motor

homes) and the road is closed during winter.

Cades Cove Loop is the #1 route in the park. This eleven mile loop winds its way through Cades Cove, which is the #1 destination in the park. This part of the park has the most historic buildings and some of the best mountain views with the highest wildlife sightings.

Clingman's Dome Road is the highest elevation route. Since it takes you to Clingman's Dome Observation Tower, it is a very popular route. It begins at the Newfound Gap parking area and ends at the park's highest elevation of 6,644 feet. You can access the Appalachian Trail from this road, as well as Andrew's Bald. This

route is closed from December 1 –
March 31.

Cataloochee Valley Road is on the
NC side of the park. Along the way
you will enjoy seeing historic
buildings, mountain vistas, and
wildlife, including elk that cannot be
seen from the TN side. Be warned
that the road is narrow and unpaved.
This is a 45-minute drive and is less
populated than other drives if you're
looking for lesser visited areas.
**Balsam Mountain Heintooga Ridge
Road** is a bit confusing because it is
called Balsam Mountain Road on
NPS maps but the road signage calls it
Heintooga Ridge. This unpaved road
extends for fourteen miles and during
that short ride descends more than
3,500 feet. If you're looking for a

lesser visited area that is still scenic,
this is it.

Two Best Day Drives in the Smokies
If you're looking for a day trip, here
are two excellent routes.

**Great Smoky Mountains National
Park Loop** covers a distance of 141
miles. It averages five hours but really
depends on how often and how long
you stop. This route includes the
Foothills Parkway, Newfound Gap
Road, The Dragon, and Little River
Road.

**The Dragon and Cherohala Skyway
Loop** is a 124-mile route. It average
three hours and includes Nantahala
National Forest, Cherokee National

Forest, and Joyce Kilmer Memorial
Forest.

<u>Four Favorite Motorcycle Routes</u>

Tail of the Dragon (US-129) is said
to be one of the most famous
motorcycle rides in America.
Covering eleven miles the road
includes 318 curves so get geared up
for an exciting ride! Fortunately, the
road is closed to commercial vehicles
and there are no intersecting roads or
driveways.

Little River Road and Newfound Gap includes the Cades Cove Loop Road, which is a highlight of the park. It climbs 3,500 feet in elevation and connects Gatlinburg, TN to Cherokee, NC.

Blue Ridge Parkway extends 469 miles through the Southern Appalachian Mountains so you'll want to enjoy only part of the route.

Cherohala Skyway is a 23-mile route that connects Tellico Plains, TN to Robbinsville, NC. Along the way you will climb as high as 5,400 feet and enjoy Cherokee National Forest and Nantahala National Forest.

FYI: The Foothills Parkway is also a popular motorcycle ride.

What to See & Do in the Park

Historic Buildings: Great Smoky
Mountains National Park holds one of
the best collections of log structures
in the eastern U.S. with more than 90
historic houses, barns, outbuildings,
churches, schools, and gristmills. All

have been preserved or restored. The best places to see them are at Cades Cove, Cataloochee, Oconaluftee, and along the Roaring Fork Motor Nature Trail. Self-guiding auto tour booklets are available at each place.

Mountain Farm Museum (Cherokee, NC) is a collection of farm buildings accumulated here from various locations throughout the park, including a log house, farmhouse, barn, apple house, springhouse, and a working blacksmith shop. Most of the structures were built in the late 19th century and were moved here in the 1950s. The museum is adjacent to the Oconaluftee Visitor Center. A half-mile north of the Oconaluftee Visitor Center is Mingus Mill. https://www.nps.gov/grsm/planyourvisit/mfm.htm

The Fairy House is actually the springhouse at what was once the Voorheis Estate, a 38-acre site a mile or so from Gatlinburg. Louis Voorheis bought the land in 1928. He used the two creeks that ran across the

property for a water-powered
mill. He even built a hydroelectric
dam. Mr. Voorheis later deeded the
property over to the National Park
Service. Much of the original estate
still exists, including the main house,
two guest cabins, a horse barn, and an
apple barn.

To get there you, hike the Twin
Creeks Trail, a moderate trail of about
4.5 miles round trip. Park at the Ogle
Place Parking Area and walk up the
road a short ways to the trail. After
you pass the Resource Center, you
will see a small path that takes you to
the Fairy House. You will see an
arched wall with an open door and
stairs leading to the top. Visitors are
permitted inside. The moss-covered

stone walls give the appearance of a
place built for fairies or sprites.

Horseback Riding: Guided
horseback rides are available in the
park from mid-March through late
November. Rides on scenic park trails
last from 45 minutes to a few hours,
depending on which option you
choose. https://www.nps.gov/grsm/pl
anyourvisit/horseriding.htm

You can bring your own horse(s) to
the park but you must stay on

designated horse trails.
https://www.nps.gov/grsm/planyourvi
sit/maps.htm
There are hayrides, wagon rides, and
carriage rides available,
https://www.nps.gov/grsm/planyourvi
sit/horseriding.htm

Picnicking. Picnic areas are located at
Big Creek, Chimneys, Cades Cove,
Collins Creek, Cosby, Deep Creek,
Greenbrier, Heintooga, Look Rock,
Metcalf  Bottoms, and
Twin Creeks. Park
maps show where
all the picnic areas
are located. The
picnic areas at Cades Cove, Deep
Creek, Greenbrier, and Metcalf
Bottoms remain open year-round. The
remaining picnic areas are closed

during the winter.
https://www.nps.gov/grsm/planyourvi
sit/maps.htm

Wildflower Walks

There are ten great nature walks.

Appalachian Trail

The two-mile trail between Newfound
Gap and Road Prong Trail has good
viewing for late spring wildflowers
from (April & May. Park at
Newfound Gap and look for the trail
sign.

Cove Hardwood Nature Trail is
perfect for those looking for the

shortest walk. It is a three-quarter of a mile loop trail with some of the best spring wildflower viewing in the entire park. The trailhead is at Chimneys Picnic Area, which is 4.5 miles south of Sugarlands Visitor Center on the Newfound Gap Road (US-441).

Deep Creek Trail easy two-mile walk that begins at the end of the Deep Creek Road (1/2 mile beyond the Deep Creek Campground turnoff), which is north of Bryson City (follow the signs through downtown Bryson). The walk includes two waterfalls, Indian Creek and Tom Branch.

Gregory Ridge Trail is a moderately difficult walk so you may just want to

do the first couple of miles, which
offers the best wildflower viewing
anyway. To get there, take Cades
Cove Loop Road just past the Cable
Mill area. Turn onto Forge Creek
Road and follow it to the end.

Kanati Fork Trail is also a
moderately difficult walk upwards for
three miles before climbs intersecting
with the Thomas Divide Trail on
Thomas Ridge. You can turn around
after a mile and still have seen a good
many wildflowers. The Kanati Fork
Trail begins about 1/8 mile north of
the Kephart Prong footbridge on the
Newfound Gap Road (US-441),
which is eight miles north of
Oconaluftee Visitor Center.

Little River Trail is an easy two-mile
walk along scenic Little River. The

trail begins just before you enter
Elkmont Campground. If you keep
going on the Cucumber Gap and
Jakes Creek trails, you will complete
a five mile (loop) hike.

Middle Prong Trail includes
wildflowers and waterfalls.
The two-mile trail starts at the end of
Tremont Road, which begins just west
of the Townsend "Y."

Oconaluftee River Trail is an easy,
riverside walk totaling three miles
beginning at the Oconaluftee Visitor
Center, which is two miles north of
Cherokee, NC on US-441.

Porters Creek Trail is best for early
spring wildflowers (March & April).
The trail starts in the Greenbrier area
(follow highway US-321 about six
miles east of Gatlinburg). Wildflower

viewing is best during the first mile or so of the trail.

Schoolhouse Gap Trail is an easy 2.2 mile walk from Laurel Creek Road to School House Gap. This route includes a good variety of wildflowers, including some unique species. The trailhead is 3.9 miles west of the Townsend "Y" on the road to Cades Cove.

For more trail and flower details, https://www.nps.gov/grsm/learn/nature/wildflower-walks.htm

Each spring, the park hosts the **Spring Wildflower Pilgrimage**. This a week-long festival includes many programs, guided walks and hikes throughout the park. https://www.wildflowerpilgrimage.org/

Hiking. Here are some of the five most popular hikes in the park. Routes are on the park maps:

- **Charlies Bunion**
- **Alum Cave Bluffs**
- **Andrews Bald**
- **Rainbow Falls**
- **Chimney Tops**

Reservations and permits are required for all overnight stays in the park's backcountry, if you want to do backcountry hiking. https://www.nps.gov/grsm/planyourvisit/maps.htm

Biking. Bicycles are allowed on most roads within the park. It is clearly marked where they are not allowed. You should consider that many park roads are not well suited for riding

due to heavy traffic and narrow roads.
The State of Tennessee requires that
children age 16 and under wear a
helmet, but all park riders should wear
helmets and reflective gear.

There are no mountain biking trails in
Great Smoky Mountains National
Park. The Gatlinburg Trail,
the Oconaluftee River Trail, and the
lower Deep Creek Trail are the only
park trails on which bicycles are
allowed. Bicycles are prohibited on
all other park trails.

Cades Cove Loop Road is the best
place to bike ride, despite it being one
of the busiest roads in the park.
Bicyclists will enjoy the 11-mile
scenic route, including wildlife and
historic buildings.

Other areas most suitable for
bicyclists include the roads in the
Greenbrier and Tremont areas in
Tennessee, and the Cataloochee
Valley and Lakeview Drive in North
Carolina. These are marked on the
park maps.

During summer and fall, bicycles can
be rented at the campground store
(located near Cades Cove
Campground).

https://www.nps.gov/grsm/planyourvi
sit/maps.htm

Fishing: Great Smoky Mountains National Park has 2,900 miles of streams and is one of the last wild trout habitats in the eastern United States. Roughly one-fifth of the park's streams are big enough to support trout populations.

Fishing is permitted in all streams year-round in the park, from 30 minutes before official time of sunrise to 30 minutes after official time of sunset.

To fish in the Great Smoky Mountains National Park, **you need a**

valid Tennessee or North Carolina fishing license. Licenses can be obtained from the Tennessee Government Website or the North Carolina Wildlife Resources Commission. The best places are:

- Fontana Lake (best bass fishing in the park)
- Little Pigeon River (good trout fishing)
- Abrams Creek (best rainbow trout and small-mouth bass fishing in the park)
- Hazel Creek (best trout fishing in the park)
- Anthony Creek www.nps.gov/grsm/planyourvisit/fishing.htm

Wildlife viewing. This is a highlight of the park for sure, especially the black bears!

The Great Smoky Mountains National Park is home to:

- 65 species of **mammals**
- 67 native **fish species**,
- 80 types of **reptiles** and **amphibians**
- 200 species of **birds (**85 of those migrate from the neotropics and around 120 species nest here).

- 1,700 **black bears**
- Highlights: **white-tailed deer, red wolves, elk, red and gray foxes, wild boars, bobcats, river otters, groundhogs, wild turkeys**, and more.

Seeing wildlife in the Smokies can be challenging because most of the park is dense forest and especially the wolves and bobcats are shy and elusive. During winter, wildlife is more visible because trees have lost their leaves. Also, open areas, **Cataloochee** and **Cades Cove,** offer the best chances to see wildlife.

Roaring Fork Motor Nature Trail is one of the best roads to see wildlife is you have mobility issues or just prefer to drive and look. Speed limits make motorists travel at a slow pace and sightings of bear and other wildlife are sometimes seen.

Just like on an African safari, the best time to see wildlife in this park is early in the morning and in the evening. Bring binoculars or use your camera's telephoto lens for better results.

Bird watching. There are four bird watching trails in Great Smoky Mountains National Park (marked on the park map). The longest bird watching trail in the park is **Balsam Mountain Loop from Pine Oak Gap**. This trail is sixteen miles long.

Clingmans Dome is also a good place to see birds because of the high elevation. According to National Geographic, some of the breeding species that can be spotted around Clingmans Dome include:

- Common Raven
- Black-capped Chickadee
- Canada Warbler
- Brown Creeper
- Dark-eyed Junco
- Golden-crowned Kinglet
- Northern Saw-whet Owl

- Red-breasted Nuthatch
- Winter Wren

Newfound Gap Road and **Clingmans Dome Road** are also great for viewing the northern birds of the Smoky Mountains. The **parking lot at Newfound Gap** is a favorite destination for bird watchers.

The National Audubon Society has a complete listing with photos of all these species on their site, https://www.audubon.org/climate/national-parks/great-smoky-mountains-national-park

FYI: Parrot Mountain and Gardens (Pigeon Forge) is a four-acre tropical garden full of tropical birds and thousands of flowers, plants, and trees.
www.parrotmountainandgardens.com

The laws protecting park wildlife state that "Willfully approaching within 50 yards (150 feet), or any distance that disturbs or displaces bear or elk is prohibited." In addition, feeding, touching, teasing, frightening, or intentionally disturbing wildlife is prohibited. These laws are to protect both you and the wildlife.

FYI: The symbol of the Smokies, the American Black Bear, is the most popular park resident. Great Smoky Mountains National Park provides the largest protected bear habitat in the East. It is believed there are around 1,700 bears in the park, so that is roughly two bears per every square mile. (Depending on the source, there are 1,400 – 1,900 bears in the park).

Bear Facts

- Bears inhabit all elevations of the park. Black bears in the Smokies are black in color, but in other parts of the country they may be brown or cinnamon.
- They may be six feet in length and up to three feet high at the shoulder.
- During the summer months, a typical adult male bear weighs 250 pounds while adult females are only 100 pounds or so. However, bears weighing over 600 pounds have been documented in the park.
- Bears can live 12-15 years or more, but bears that have had access to human foods and garbage have a life expectancy

of only half that amount of time.

FYI: For these reasons, park rangers issue citations for littering, feeding bears, and for improper food storage. These citations can result in fines of up to $5,000 and jail sentences lasting up to six months. Dispose of all garbage or food scraps in bear proof garbage containers or take it with you. Do not feed wildlife. Use the food storage cables to store your food and garbage when camping in the backcountry.

- Bears, like humans, are omnivores. Plant materials like berries, insects, and nuts make up 85% of their diet. Bears have color vision and a keen sense of smell.
- They are good tree climbers, can swim very well, and can run 30 miles per hour! Never try to outrun a bear. By the way, bear attacks in the park are extremely rare
- Mating takes place in July and bears may have more than one mate.
- Bear sightings in the park are most common during the early morning (6-10am) and evening hours (3-7pm) in spring and summer when they are the most active. The

best place for bear sightings
is in Cades Cove.

- Bears hide in a "denning site"
  when the weather turns cold.
  Dens are hollow stumps, tree
  cavities, caves, or wherever
  there is shelter. Bears in the
  Smokies are unusual in that
  they often den high above the
  ground in standing hollow
  trees.

- Bears do not truly hibernate,
  but enter long periods of sleep.
  They may leave the den for
  short periods if disturbed or
  during brief warming trends.

- One to four cubs are born
  during the mother's winter
  sleep, usually in late January or
  early February. Bears weigh
  eight ounces at birth.

- Females with newly born cubs
  usually emerge from their
  winter dens in late March or
  early April. Commonly born in
  pairs, the cubs will remain with
  the mother for about eighteen
  months or until she mates
  again.

What Should I Do If I See A Bear?

If you see a bear:

- Do not approach it
- Do not allow the bear to approach you.
- If your presence causes the bear to change its behavior (stops eating, changes its direction, etc.) you are TOO close.

- Being too close may promote aggressive behavior from the bear because he/she perceives you as a threat. If the bear moves towards you, makes loud noises, or moves its paws as in swatting gestures, the bear is demanding more space. Slowly back away while watching the bear. Increase the distance between you and the bear. The bear will most likely do the same.

If a bear persistently approaches you, without making loud noises or paw swatting:

- Change your direction.
- If the bear continues to follow you, stand your ground.

- If the bear gets closer, shout at it. In other words, act aggressively to intimate the bear.
- Throw non-food objects such as rocks at the bear.
- Use a deterrent such as a big stick.
- If you are carrying bear spray, begin to discharge it when the bear comes within 15-20 yards of you.
- Don't discharge a firearm; this can cause a safety hazard for other visitors. Also, it is illegal to shoot a bear in the park.

SUMMARY:
**The National Park Service is
serious about protecting its bears.
You are a visitor in their home.
Respect them.
Keep food and garbage secure.
Keep your distance from bears,
especially cubs (where you see cubs,
mamas are nearby).
Never run!**

Two Places You Have to Visit in the Park

1. Clingman's Dome

At 6,643 feet, Clingmans Dome is the highest point in the Great Smoky Mountains National Park. In fact, it is the highest point in Tennessee, and the third highest mountain east of the Mississippi.

The observation tower on the summit of Clingmans Dome offers spectacular 360° views for visitors willing to climb the steep half-mile to the tower at the top. It is FREE to go onto the observation tower.

Clouds, rain, and cold temperatures are common at Clingmans Dome. Temperatures at the dome are 10-20 degrees cooler than in lower elevations, so dress accordingly.

The road leading to the tower is closed seasonally (usually from early December through late March), and any other times that weather conditions mandate it too dangerous.

On a clear day, you can see up to 100 miles so you can see seven states from the top of the tower!
(Clockwise: Tennessee, Kentucky,

Virginia, North Carolina, South
Carolina, Georgia and Alabama.)

The best time to visit Clingmans
Dome is in the morning for sunrise
and before the crowds or at sunset.
Also, at this time of day you may see
bears on the walk up!

Pets and bicycles are not permitted on
the paved trail to the observation
tower or on any other trails in the
area. There is a bike rack and you can
secure your bike if you bring a lock.
While the trail to the summit is paved,
it is too steep for wheelchairs.

Directions: Turn off Newfound Gap
Road 0.1 mile south of Newfound
Gap and follow the 7-mile-long
Clingmans Dome Road (with scenic
pull-offs along the way) to the large

parking area at the end. From there, it
is a half-mile paved walk to the tower.

2. Cades Cove

Easily the most popular thing to do in Cades Cove is drive/ride/walk the 11-mile scenic loop road to the dozens of historic structures (including cabins, barns, mills, homesteads, and churches) and scenic overlooks. Allow 2 – 4 hours to explore Cades Cove (or longer if you walk some of the area's trails). Traffic is heavy in the summer and fall and on weekends year-round.

Admission is free. A self-guiding auto tour booklet is available for a small fee at the loop road entrance.

FYI: Vehicle-Free Day is all day Wednesdays from the first Wednesday in May to the last Wednesday to provide opportunities for pedestrians and cyclists to experience Cades Cove without motor vehicles.

The visitor center (halfway around the 11-mile loop) features both indoor and outdoor exhibits detailing

Southern mountain life. Visit the
Cable Mill, a grist mill that operates
in the spring, summer and fall, and the
historic Becky Cable House, or
explore the exhibits inside the center.
Several ranger-led programs are
available seasonally and the visitor
center offers a bookstore, public
restrooms and trail maps for hikers.

Five Best Things to See in Cades Cove

1. One secret spot you'll have to get out of your car to find is The **Pearl Harbor Tree**. Golman Myers planted the tree as a tribute to all those who lost their lives during Pearl Harbor. His son, Bernard, came back to

the area in the 1970s and placed a metal tag on the tree that reads, "Golman Myers transplanted this tree Dec. 7, 1941." Directions: Drive 3.5 miles down the road until you're 0.5 mile away from Missionary Baptist Church. You'll walk into the tree line headed west for about 0.1 mile, and there's a clearing on the left side of the road. Keep walking towards the treeline along the western edge of the field and climb up the hill to get to the tree.

2. **Abrams Falls** is a
    beautiful waterfall in the
    Cades Cove area of the
    park. From November to
    April, the cove is open to
    vehicle traffic at all
    times. During this period,
    it's best to arrive early to
    beat the crowds. Arriving
    in Cades Cove before 9
    a.m. most days will give
    you plenty of time to
    explore the valley
    without running into
    large groups of people.

Abrams Falls has a deep swimming hole that attracts visitors between late spring and early fall. The swimming hole is about 100 feet wide in all directions, so swimmers have plenty of room to swim on even the busiest of days.

3. **Gregory's Cave** is an underground cave located in Cades Cove. This is a natural cave that

was used for mining in the pioneer days. It eventually became a tourist attraction in the 1920s by the Gregory family, but it was closed after they moved out of the area. While you can't enter the cave, you are able to see inside the mouth of the cave. Drive along the Loop until you reach John Oliver Cabin. There will be a dirt road with metal bars blocking it on the right. Hike along this road until you see a small picnic area on the right and the cave is a short distance ahead.

4. **The Cantilever Barn**

This type of structure is unique to
Sevier County, Tennessee, so you
won't find them anywhere else.
Historians believe the farmers in the
area combined two European barn
designs to create this barn. Livestock
and crops were kept here to stay dry
and secure. It is located on the second
half of the Cades Cove Loop.

5. **Gourley's Pond**

One secret spot you'll definitely want
to try to find after a good rainfall is
Gourley's Pond. It is a wet weather
pond, so only worth the visit if there
has been rain recently. Not much
here, but it is a nice little pond in a
quiet, natural area. To get to the pond,
park at the LeQuire Cemetery past the
south end of Sparks Lane. Walk along
the road about 200 feet until you see
the path on the right. Follow the path
for 100 feet and then go southwest
until you see the pond.

**FYI:** *Beware!* **While
there are two dozen
species of snakes in
the park, only two are poisonous:
Northern Copperhead and
Timberwood Rattlesnake.**

Hiking

There are several trails in Cades Cove, including the five-mile roundtrip trail to Abrams Falls and the short Cades Cove Nature Trail. Longer hikes to Thunderhead Mountain and Rocky Top also begin in the cove. Also, there are several Deep Creek hikes to choose from: Juney Whank Falls (0.6 mile), Three Waterfalls Loop (2.4 miles), and Deep Creek-Indian Creek Loop (4.4 miles). Longer loop hikes are also possible. Trails to the waterfalls start from the large parking area at the end of Deep Creek Road (across the creek from Deep Creek Campground).

Deep Creek is also known for its all-season outdoor activities—swimming, skiing, boating, snowboarding, tubing, biking, and rafting. Mule deer, elk, mountain lion, and bobcat are the larger animals that make a home here.

 Whether hiking or driving, keep watch for wildlife. Cades Cove is one of the best wildlife viewing areas of the park.

Best Trails for Strollers & Scooters

Sugarlands Valley Nature Trail is a paved ½ mile loop that is just south of the Sugarlands Visitor Center. There is parking at the trailhead and the route is scenic and you just might see wildlife along the way.

Gatlinburg Trail is a 1.9 mile one-way trail that begins at the Sugarlands Visitor Center and goes to the outskirts of Gatlinburg. The trail is flat and includes a pedestrian footbridge. It runs through the forest by the Little Pigeon River and you will see old homesites along the way.

Clingmans Dome Observation Tower Trail isn't suitable for wheelchairs but you can push a stroller up the ½ mile paved trail if you have a bit of muscle.

Laurel Falls Trail is a 2.6-mile round-trip trail that is one of the most popular places in the park with an 80-foot-tall waterfall and a footbridge in front for taking photos.

FYI: To get the latest alerts (trail and weather advisories, road closures, etc.),
https://www.nps.gov/grsm/planyour visit/

Best Waterfalls in the Park

- **Rainbow Falls** is the tallest *single-drop* falls in the park. When it's sunny out, the mist from the falls creates a beautiful rainbow. It's 5.4 mile round trip hike.

- **Ramsey Cascades** is the tallest *overall* at 100 feet. An eight-mile hike is required to see these falls and it is considered to be a difficult hike.

- **Grotto Falls** is a 25-foot waterfall in the middle of a Hemlock forest. It is an easy 2.5 mile round trip hike where you'll see wildflowers on the way and salamanders when you get there.

- **Laurel Falls** is one of the most popular waterfalls in the whole park. To reach the falls, you'll hike 2.6 miles (round trip).
- **The Sinks** is a waterfall right off Little River Road. No hiking is required! The Sinks is about 12 miles west of Sugarland Visitor Center.
- **Meigs Falls** is another roadside waterfall along Little River Road. No hiking is necessary! The falls are 13 miles west of Sugarlands Visitor Center.
- **Place of 1,000 Drips**: Find these falls along the Roaring Fork Motor Nature Trail during the rainy season. The names come from the way the falls split into many different "drips" that flow over lovely moss-covered rocks.

- **Mingo Falls** is technically outside of the National Park on the Cherokee Reservation, but well worth a visit. At 120 feet tall, this waterfall is one of tallest in the southern Appalachians. The hike to the falls is 1/2 mile each way on the Pigeon Creek Trail, which originates at Mingo Falls Campground.

 Waterfalls are all over the park. See a park map for more locations.

https://nps.gov/grsm/planyourvisit/maps.htm

Accommodations

LeConte Lodge is the *only lodging inside the Great Smoky Mountains National Park.* At 6,593 feet, Mount LeConte is the third tallest peak in the park and home to one of the most unique backcountry accommodations in the National Park System, LeConte Lodge. Built in 1926, this backcountry lodge is comprised of

seven log cabins and three lodges
with individual bedrooms and a
communal dining room. You can only
get to the lodge on foot! Of the six
trails that lead to the lodge, Alum
Cave is the shortest but steepest: 5
miles one-way with nearly 3,000 feet
in elevation gain. For those looking
for a longer route (Are you crazy?),
Brushy Mountain suits the bill at 9.1
miles one-way. The most popular
route, however, tends to be Trillium
Gap at 6.7 miles. It's supposed to be
the easiest of the six trails and it is
also where hikers will likely
encounter the lodge's llama supply
train on Mondays, Wednesdays and

Fridays when supplies are brought in.

Food and all other supplies for lodge

guests must be packed in. Llamas

have the least environmental impact,

so they are used for deliveries.

You'll learn to really appreciate the

kerosene lamps and propane heaters

since there's no electricity at the

lodge. Towels and linens are

provided, but there no showers at the lodge. Thankfully, there are flush toilets in an adjacent privy building. A delicious, hearty dinner is served in the cozy dining room.

The view of the sunrise from Myrtle Point is stunning. Water and pack lunches are available for day hikers, along with merchandise from the camp store. Plan well in advance if you'd like to stay here because the lodge sells out quickly!

www.lecontelodge.com/reservations/

You can utilize the usual rental resources, such as **Expedia, VRBO, Airbnb, Booking, and Trivago,** but there are some exceptional local rental companies you should also consider:

Smoky Mountain Cabin & Condo Rentals, https://smokymountains.com/
Aunt Bug's Cabin Rentals, www.auntbug.com
Natural Retreats, https://www.naturalretreats.com/great-smoky-mountains-cabin-rentals
Cabins of the Smokies, https://www.cabinsofthesmokymountains.com/
Pigeon Forge Cabin Rentals, https://www.pigeonforge.com/stay-a-while/pigeon-forge-cabin-rentals/
For more listings: https://smokymountainnationalpark.com/lodging/

TENNESSEE GATEWAY CITIES

Gatlinburg

Gatlinburg is the closest town to the park. It is just outside the Sugarlands entrance to the Great Smoky Mountains National Park.

With a population of roughly 4,000, visitors often outnumber residents. And vehicles often overcrowd the town's roads and parking lots. It is best to park and walk.

FYI: The Gatlinburg Trolley can also be used as an easy way to get into downtown. Use the Park-n-Ride Lot at the Gatlinburg Welcome Center (1011 Banner Road, just off of the Spur before town) board a trolley and be in downtown Gatlinburg within minutes. So easy and convenient!

The **Gatlinburg Trolley** is free and fun! It runs 365 days a year. There are stops all over town and you can get on and off as you please. All trolleys stop at the Mass Transit Center, which is located at Ripley's Aquarium.

Hours of Operation

March - April:
10:30 a.m. - 10 p.m.

May - October:
8:30 a.m. - 12 midnight

November - February:
Sunday - Thursday 10:30 a.m. - 6 p.m.
Fridays and Saturdays 10:30 a.m. - 10 p.m.

The Trolley System operates three routes. The **Red Route** begins at Ripley's Aquarium and services River Road, a portion of Ski Mountain Road, the Parkway from Traffic Light No. 10 to Traffic Light No. 8, the Airport Road Area, the Park Vista Hotel, Cherokee Orchard Road, Baskins Creek Road, Woliss Lane, before returning to Parkway at Traffic Light No. 6.

The **Purple Route** includes the Gatlinburg Welcome Center, Westgate Resorts and the Parkway between Traffic Lights Nos. 1 and 5. The **Blue Route** serves East Gatlinburg along U.S. Highway 321 and the Parkway between Traffic Lights Nos. 3 and 5.
https://www.gatlinburg.com/trolley/routesfares/

Parking. The city offers FREE Park
and Ride lots. These lots are located
at the Gatlinburg Welcome Center
and the City Hall Complex on
Highway 321. Paid parking lots are
also available with daily rates.

Gatlinburg Dining. It can be pricey
to eat in Gatlinburg, especially dinner.
The best places to eat on a budget are
Slice Pizza Bakery, Mama's Chicken
Kitchen, Parton's Deli, and Tennessee
Jed's.
More expensive but worth the
splurge: Timbers Log Cabin
Restaurant, Bubba Gump Shrimp
Company, Split Rail Eats, and Cliff
Top Restaurant at Anakeesta. There
are fudge shops, candy stores,
sandwich shops, pancake houses, and
lots of other food options scattered
throughout Gatlinburg.

Our family has been going to **The
Donut Friar** for years. They have the
best donuts, pastries, and cinnamon
bread. They also serve a good
selection of beverages, including
specialty coffees. The trick is to get
there early. They open at 5 a.m. and
are mostly sold out by 11 a.m.
Located at The Village Shoppes.

If you're looking for a special spot,
The Greenbrier is it. It is a lodge-

style restaurant perched on the edge
of the park. They serve high quality
seafood and cuts of beef. Also, they
have a large selection of creative
cocktails and whiskeys.

Crockett's Breakfast Camp has the
biggest breakfast plates you've ever
seen (two can easily share one).
Seriously! The pancakes are about
two inches thick! They are known for
their pancakes and cinnamon rolls.
They are big and delicious! It's a
popular place, so if you come during
peak breakfast hours, expect to wait.

Fannie Farkle's is a fun, family
restaurant. All ages will love the
100% beef Ogle Dogs. And all ages
will enjoy their delightful arcade (and
great prizes!). They also serve
Sausage Subs, Cheesesteaks,

Hawaiian Shaved Ice, and more. Use this link to find coupons, https://fanniefarkles.com/coupons/

The Peddler steakhouse is known for their excellent cuts of beef and tasty trout, as well as their extensive salad bar. Reservations are highly recommended during peak season. 820 River Road.

Also worth mentioning... **Park Grill** and **Smoky Mountain Trout House** are also good dinner choices.

FYI: Classic Smoky Mountain foods are Tennessee BBQ, buttermilk pancakes, fresh mountain trout, Cherokee fry bread, old-fashioned taffy (you can watch them make it in Gatlinburg), and Smoky Mountain Moonshine.

Things to Do in Gatlinburg

What can't you do would be a shorter
list! There are so many options it is
almost too many choices.

For example, you can take the
Chondola to the top of **Anakeesta
Mountain** and then the possibilities
are numerous: Anavista Tower,
Treetop Skywalk, Dueling Zipline
Adventure, Rail Runner Mountain
Coaster, Gem Mining, Vista Gardens,
Astra Lumina, restaurants and shops.
www.anakeesta.com

Alpine Slides, Skating, Skiing &
Snowboarding are available at
Tennessee's only ski resort, **Ober
Gatlinburg**. It operates seasonally
from December through March. All
levels of skiers and snowboarders are

117

welcome. Tubing can be achieved in
the 9-lane snow tubing park. The
indoor skating rink is open year
round! There is also an alpine slide,
mountain coaster, and wildlife
encounter. And there are plenty of
dining and relaxing options, including
the Ober Lounge, Ober Restaurant,
and other onsite eateries.
www.obergatlinburg.com

**Ripley's Believe It or Not
Odditorium** is a favorite of mine. It
boasts more than 500 exhibits and
artifacts that are oddly interesting,
such as the collection of 100
authentic shrunken heads. But if
you're not into strange stuff,
Ripley's has eight other attractions
in the Gatlinburg area:

- **Ripley's Haunted Adventure.**
- **Ripley's 5D Moving Theater.**
- **Ripley's Marvelous Mirror Maze.**
- **Ripley's Mini-Golf.**
- **Ripley's Super Fun Zone.**
- **Ripley's Super Fun Park.**
- **Ripley's Mountain Coaster.**
- **Ripley's Aquarium of the Smokies.**

https://www.ripleys.com/gatlinburg/

Walk across the longest
pedestrian **Skybridge** in North
America. Seriously! At 680 feet long,
it is the longest pedestrian cable
bridge in North America. Also at
Skybridge, is SkyTrail, SkyCenter,
SkyLift Park, and SkyDeck.
https://www.gatlinburgskylift.com/sk
ybridge

Ride the 2.1-mile **Ober Gatlinburg Aerial Tram** to a mountaintop of fun. When you reach the end of your scenic ride, you have arrived at Ober Mountain Adventure Park & Ski Area. Activities include Ice Bumper Cars, Alpine Slide, Ice Skating, Summer Tubing or Winter Snow Tubing, Snowboarding, Cubbies Snow Zone, and much more! https://obergatlinburg.com/aerial-tramway/

Gatlinburg Space Needle thrills riders with a 400-foot ride on a glass elevator up to a 360 degree observation tower. www.gatlinburgspaceneedle.com

FYI: Gatlinburg Farmers Market is open every Saturday selling fresh local foods and crafts.

Arrowmont School of Arts and Crafts dates back more than 100 years. It has evolved to showcase the most beautiful, best handmade crafts of this region. The school also serves to teach and preserve Appalachian craft. Visitors can explore the galleries that house permanent and rotating exhibits featuring traditional Appalachian artwork.
www.arrowmont.org

Extreme Mini Golf. Take a funicular up the mountain to play your first hole. Descend the mountain as you play through crazy fun Hillbilly Golf.
https://www.gatlinburg.com/listing/hillbilly-golf/327/

More Things to Do...

Gatlin's Rugged Ropes Adventure
Course, Ripley's Moving Theater,
Gatlin's Escape Games, Ripley's
Aquarium, Gatlin's Laser Tag,
Ripley's Haunted Adventure,
Gatlinburg Axe House, Hollywood
Star Cars Museum, Salt & Pepper
Shaker Museum, Crave Golf Club,
Circus Golf, Treasure Quest Golf, and
Mysterious Mansion of Gatlinburg.

Shopping. There are shops, galleries,
and stores all over Gatlinburg. The
most popular is The Village. This is a
collection of 27 galleries, boutiques,
clothiers, and eateries (including an
Irish pub) housed in a quaint
European-themed village.

Accommodations. There are lots of chain hotels and motels in the Gatlinburg area. If you belong to a hotel loyalty program, you may want to stay at The **Park Vista by Hilton Doubletree**. Rooms can be had for 40,000 HH points. **Fairfield Inn and Suites Gatlinburg Downtown by Marriott** is a good choice for Marriott members. Breakfast is included and there is a nice outdoor firepit to enjoy on cool evenings. IHG members can get rooms at **Holiday Inn Express Gatlinburg Downtown** for 30,000 points. There is an indoor pool for year round enjoyment. Also worth mentioning is the **Greystone Lodge on the River.** It is conveniently located next to the trolley station and Ripley's Aquarium.

Best Budget Options: River Edge
Inn, Greystone Lodge on the River,
Country Inn & Suites by Radisson,
Carr's Northside Cottages & Motel,
and Zoder's Inn & Suites. Breakfast
included at all but Carr's and
Greystone. If you ask for a discount,
you will often receive one even if
you're not a member of AAA or
AARP, so be sure to ask!

**FYI: From November to February,
downtown Gatlinburg is decorated
to the hilt, resembling a winter
wonderland, as it celebrates its
annual Winterfest Celebration. And
before that, enjoy Smoky Mountain
Harvest Festival that kicks off fall
and fall colors season.**

www.gatlinburg.com

Sevierville

Sevier County Heritage Museum is located in the former Sevierville Post Office building, which is listed on the National Register of Historic Places. Displays include Native American artifacts, items from the Revolutionary War, Civil War, & World War II, and much more. FREE. It is one block from the courthouse. www.seviercountyheritagemuseum.org

Smoky Mountain Relic Room can be found inside Smoky Mountain Knife Works, "the world's largest knife showplace." The Relic Room is packed with 3.4 billion years of

history that you can see, touch and

most is for sale! Tere is no charge to

browse and explore the facility.

A lovely bronze statue of **Dolly Parton** adorns the lawn of the Sevier County Courthouse. Snap a selfie with Dolly playing her guitar while you're here! The statue has attracted millions of visitors from all over the world.

Tennessee Museum of Aviation, in Sevierville displays vintage aircraft and military vehicles. You can climb into an A-4 Skyhawk Cockpit and see all kinds of military memorabilia. The "Wave Wall" shares a timeline of aviation history milestones. $. www.tnairmuseum.com

Sevier Air Trampoline & Ninja Warrior Park is the area's largest trampoline park with five dozen trampolines, an obstacle course inspired by the popular "Ninja Warrior" TV show, two tumble tracks for gymnastics, a rope swing, a jousting area and more. www.sevierair.com

Wilderness at the Smokies Waterpark Resort & Family Adventure Center is home to Tennessee's largest indoor waterpark. Plus, there are two outdoor waterparks, Adventure Forest (25,000-square feet), a three-story ropes course, blacklight mini-golf,

huge arcade, multi-level laser tag, and

more.

www.wildernessatthesmokies.com

**NASCAR SpeedPark Smoky

Mountains** is rated as one of the top

tourist attractions in North America. It

has 25 acres filled with eight go-kart

tracks, bumper boats, amusement park

rides, a three-story climbing wall, two

miniature golf courses, arcade, and

more. www.nascarspeedpark.com

Rainforest Adventures Zoo houses

reptiles, mammals, bugs, birds, and

amphibians, such as Hedgehogs,

African Serval, Lemurs, Scorpions,
Tarantulas, and much more.

www.rfadventures.com

Tennessee Smokies is a Double-A
Affiliate of the Chicago Cubs. Enjoy a
game at Smokies Stadium, which has
been dubbed "America's Friendliest
Ballpark. Kodak, TN (8 miles from
Sevierville).

https://www.milb.com/tennessee

Duke (Is he taking bids for the

secret recipe?)

**FYI: BUSH's Visitors Center &
Museum (in nearby Chestnut Hill)
is housed in the original A.J. Bush
& Company general store, which
was founded in 1897. The Visitor
Center offers a museum, theater,**

gift shop, and café that serves Southern dishes, including the "No. 1 Baked Beans in the World" (Bush's Beans) and Pinto Bean Pie dessert. The museum screens a short film that features Jay Bush (the founder's great-grandson) and Duke (the dog who notoriously offers to reveal the secret recipe for the right price), Bush family history, and a behind-the-scenes peek at how beans are processed. Displays include a giant replica can of Bush's Baked Beans, a scale that reveals your weight in beans, and the laser-protected book with the secret recipe.

Forbidden Caves is one of many Tennessee caves (TN has more caves than anywhere else in the U.S.).

Special effects lighting can be
enjoyed during the guided tour. The
cave stays 58°F year round but is only
open seasonally. www.forbidden.com

**Smoky Mountain School of
Cooking, Appalachian Store, Café
& Classes** offers cooking classes,
shopping, and a café to enjoy
Appalachian food. The large gift shop
offers Smoky Mountain souvenirs and
Appalachian gifts.
www.smokymountainschoolofcookin
g.com

Sevierville Golf Club is a private

club that welcomes the public.

www.sevievillegolfclub.com

 **FYI: Get the new
Sevierville Savings
Pass to save big
money on lodging,
restaurants, attractions, shopping,
and more! Download at
Explore.VisitSevierville.com**

Enjoy a drink…
Apple Barn Winery
Hillside Winery
**Old Tennessee Distilling Company
(Kodak, TN)**
*There are many more area wineries
and distilleries.

135

1919 Society is a Prohibition-style speakeasy located inside an old two-story bank in downtown Sevierville.

Dining. Alamo Steakhouse (hand-cut Angus steaks, seafood & chops), Big Daddy's Pizzeria, Black Rifle Coffee Company, Chubby's Restaurant, Flapjack's Pancake Cabin, and Penny's Café, as well as fast food chains.

Shopping. Scrapbook Superstore has the largest scrapbook inventory in America. Bass Pro Outdoor World, Music Outlet, Action Antique Barn, Smoky Mountains Knife Works, Flea Traders Paradise, Gorilla Fireworks Superstore. Tanger Outlet, Boot Factory Outlet, Cherokee Trading Post, Christmas & Collectibles

(Kodak, TN), and more antiques, flea
markets, and art galleries.

FYI: Sevierville is 14 miles from Gatlinburg.

Accommodations. Lodging options
are plentiful. There are a half dozen
campgrounds and RV parks. The
newest is **Pigeon Forge Landing RV
Resort.** It has lots of amenities,
including a lazy river. 455 Lonesome
Valley Drive, Sevierville.

There are lots of motels and
hotels too. The newest is the **Historic
Central Hotel**, a boutique property in
downtown Sevierville. It offers 2 & 3-
bedrooms and rooftop dining. The
original hotel was dismantled in 1968
to make room for Sevier County
Bank. The bank was located on that
spot for almost four decades before

moving into a new building right next door in 2006.
www.thecentralhotel.com.

Clarion Inn Willow River has been newly renovated. They serve a full, hot breakfast, offer suites with fireplaces, fitness center, indoor/outdoor pools, lazy river, balcony rooms, and more.

Opening soon will be the **Davis Hotel**, another boutique hotel in downtown Sevierville.

More options: The Resort at Governor's Crossing, Holiday Inn Express & Suites, Hampton Inn Sevierville, The Inn at Apple Valley, Fairfield Inn & Suites by Marriott, and Baymont Inn & Suites.

Sevierville has lots of standard lodging options, but if you're *looking for something a bit nicer…*

Berry Spring Lodge

Blue Mountain Mist Country Inn & Cottages

The Ridge Outdoor Resort

Oak Haven Resort & Spa

Hidden Mountain Resort

Wilderness at the Smokies is a resort with a giant waterpark. The property offers different types of lodging, including Stone Hill Lodge, River Lodge Suites, and villas. The adventure park includes waterslides, a massive Adventure Forest, laser tag, arcade, and more! Resort guests enjoy the waterpark and adventure park at no extra cost. To make reservations, https://www.wildernessatthesmokies.com/

Sanctuary Treehouse Resort claims to be the world's largest treehouse resort. It is an interactive treehouse resort situated on forty acres with views of two championship golf courses and panoramic views of the Smoky Mountains.
www.treehouseresort.com

There are lots of cabin rentals available,
https://visitsevierville.com/lodging-cabins

Sevierville Chamber of Commerce Visitors Center is located at 3099 Winfield Dunn Parkway, Kodak, TN.
www.visitsevierville.com

Pigeon Forge

Pigeon Forge, also on the Tennessee side of the park, is a short 8-mile drive north of Gatlinburg. It has the most to offer of the communities surrounding the park.

Its top attraction is **Dollywood**, which has been voted the #1 theme park in the U.S. by TripAdvisor. The theme park has 50+ rides, entertainment, and dining options. Some of the top rides are Lightning Rod (the world's fastest wooden roller coaster), Mystery Mine, Blazing Fury, Barnstormer, Daredevil Falls, and Thunderhead.

Big Bear Mountain is the park's newest and longest roller coaster. It has a top speed of 48mph and passes behind a waterfall! The park is open seasonally. www.dollywood.com

Seasonal Celebrations at Dollywood

I Will Always Love You (March/April)

Flower & Food Festival (April – June)

Smoky Mountain Summer Celebration (June – August)

Great Pumpkin LumiNights at Dollywood (September – November)

Dollywood's Harvest Festival (September – November)

Smoky Mountain Christmas
(November – January)

Doggies & Dollywood. Dogs are not allowed in the park but can board them at Dollywood's day kennels for a small fee. Doggywood has spacious and cozy Kennel Runs, as well as a few cottages for dogs that require more privacy. Reservations are recommended because space is limited. Water is always available but you must bring dog food if you would like your pet to be fed during the day. https://www.dollywood.com/themepa rk/guest-services/doggywood/

 **FYI: For more pet-friendly places and things to do with your pets in Pigeon Forge,** https://www.mypigeonforge.com/blog/dog-friendly-things-to-do-in-pigeon-forge

More Dolly Parton Attractions…

Dollywood's Splash Country has been voted a Top 10 Outdoor Waterpark by *USA Today* Readers. www.dollywood.com

Dolly Parton's Stampede features 4-course feast followed by a show with music, comedy, live animals &

144

pyrotechnics.

https://dpstampede.com/pigeon-forge

Pirates Voyage Dinner & Show is the newest Dolly Parton attraction in Pigeon Forge. During the show, pirates battle on land, on ship, in the water, and high in the air above their pirate ships! The show features acrobatics, live animals, and competitions. It includes a four-course feast with dessert. Arrive early and you can get photo ops of your kids made over into pirates or mermaids at Pirate Village.
https://piratesvoyage.com/pigeon-forge/

FYI: The pirate show is great entertainment for kids and adults—or at least I enjoyed it, including their special Christmas-themed pirate show!

The next biggest attraction in Pigeon Forge is the **Titanic Museum Attraction**. This is a 30,000 square foot replica of the *Titanic*. The museum was built with actual *Titanic* blueprints at a cost of

$25 million. The museum holds 400 pre-discovery artifacts in twenty galleries. As guests enter, they are given a passenger boarding ticket. On this ticket is the name of an actual *Titanic* passenger and the class they were traveling. Guests will learn the individual stories of several passengers. In the *Titanic* Memorial Room, they will find out whether their ticketed passenger survived.

www.titanicpigeonforge.com

More Attractions: Alcatraz East Crime Museum, Smoky Mountain Alpine Coaster, Hollywood Wax Museum, Wonderworks Pigeon Forge, The Island at Pigeon Forge,

MagiQuest, Ripley's Aquarium, Pigeon Forge Snow, Top Jump Trampoline Park & Extreme Arena, Legacy Mountain Ziplines, Island Bumper Cars, Paula Deen Lumberjack Adventure Park & Lumberjack Feud Show, and Anakeesta. Battleground Tactical Laser Tag, Xtreme Racing Center, Rowdy Bear Ridge, and The Island Ropes Course.

New! **Toy Box Mini Golf** is the world's first toy-themed miniature golf course. There is also a laser maze and toy store on site. www.toyboxgolf.com

Looking for more adventure?

Outdoor Gravity Park

Flyaway Indoor Skydiving

Exorent ATV & Dune Buggy Rentals

Smoky Mountains Outdoor
Whitewater Rafting

Wranglers & Razors Pigeon Forge
Jeep & UTV Rentals

Scenic Helicopter Tours

Pink Jeep Tours

Pigeon Forge Axe House

SkyFly: Soar America is a new flying
theater that offers a fully immersive
experience where guests fly over
some of the most iconic locations in
the U.S.

Tours & Entertainment: Moonshine & Wine Tour (half-day tour of 3 distilleries & 3 wineries), Hatfield & McCoy Dinner Show, Comedy Barn Theater, Great Smoky Mountain Murder Mystery Dinner Show, Dolly Parton's Stampede, Pirates Voyage Dinner Show, and Country Tonite Theatre. Also, there are movie theaters, axe (throwing) taverns, escape rooms, arcades, kids adventure parks, outlet malls, and more!

Parks. Patriot Park and Wear Farm City Park are nice spots to enjoy a little R & R. **Patriot Park** is dog-friendly and is right by the Old Mill. There is a ½ mile loop trail that runs along the river. Along the path there are flags from all 50 states and other memorials dedicated to Pigeon Forge vets. **Wear Farm City Park** is

another dog-friendly park with a few
trails to choose from and playground
area. Additionally, there are picnic
shelters, restrooms, parking, and
sports fields.

Shopping. Pigeon Forge is home to
300 outlets, boutiques, shops, and
stores, including Mountain Mile &
Tower Shops, The Island, Three Bears
General Store, Island Trading
Company, The Toy Chest, and The
Shops of Pigeon Forge.

Mountain Mile & Tower Shops is
huge, spanning 175 acres! It has
dining, shopping, and entertainment
venues. The Lawn is a large outdoor
space with firepits and seating areas.
There's even a life-size chessboard
you can play.

**FYI: Don't miss the dancing
fountains at The Island in Pigeon
Forge. Get comfy in a rocking chair
and watch the fountain come to life!
The light and music show takes
place every half hour.**

There are lots of restaurants, fast
food, bars, and cafes. The best place
to listen to live music is at **The
Listening Room Café**. It features
indoor and outdoor seating and a large
stage. Two full-service bars serve an
extensive cocktail list. But for the best
margaritas, go to **No Way Jose's
Mexican Cantina.**

More good places to eat and drink:
The Casual Pint, PizzaRio Wine &
Bar, Blue Moose Burgers & Wings,
Old Mill Pottery House Café & Grill,

Wild Bear Tavern, Alamo
Steakhouse, Huck Finn's Catfish
Cabin, and The Local Goat.

Best Eats on a Budget: Lil' Black
Bear Café, Smokies Cuban Café,
Mama's Farmhouse, Mel's Diner, and
Cookie Dough Monster Burgers &
Shakes. Pigeon Forge Deli is a good
place to pick up picnic fixings.

**FYI: Trolley buses connect the
cities of Pigeon Forge, Gatlinburg
and Sevierville**, and are extremely
convenient and affordable to cruise
around in an air conditioned vehicle,
take in the views and be served by the
quaint, blast-from-the-past-yet-ultra-
modern trolley service.

Accommodations. Dollywood's DreamMore Resort & Spa offers pools, kids activities, full service salon & spa, restaurant, store, shopping, fitness center, and more. www.dollywood.com/resort

Bear Cove Cabins is the preferred Smoky Mountain Cabin Rental Company for Dollywood Parks and Resorts. Bear Cove Cabins allow you to choose what Smoky Mountain cabin best suits your family. www.dollywood.com/cabins

New! **Dollywood's HeartSong Lodge & Resort** welcomes you into the 4,000 sq. ft. four-story atrium lobby where a huge stone fireplace and lantern-inspired windows create the perfect ambience. Choose from rooms or suites with or without balconies. There is a full-service restaurant staffed by a chef, lounge, private dining room, and Songbird Market Grab & Go eatery. Honeysuckle & Pine Storied Goods Mercantile offers essentials, souvenirs, and more. www.dollywood.com/heartsong/

Parrot Mountain Cabins are less than one mile from Dollywood. Cabins include cable TV and high-speed internet. www.parrotmountaincabins.com

More Pigeon Forge Lodging. ($ - $$$$)
The Inn at Christmas Place
The Inn on the River Pigeon Forge
Great Smokies Resort Lodge
Quality Inn & Suites Dollywood
Park Grove Inn
Creekstone Inn

Microtel Inn & Suites by Wyndham
Pigeon Forge
Timbers Lodge

AUTHOR'S NOTE: I recommend staying in a cabin rather than a hotel. They provide more of a "mountain experience" than staying at a chain hotel. They offer more privacy, a kitchen, and laundry facilities. That said, some people prefer the hotel experience for security and convenience. One caveat if you do opt for a cabin, is to make sure where it is located. Some are on the top of mountains that require long drives full of hairpin curves with no guardrails and many of these roads are not paved (gravel) so in the snow or rain they can be a bit treacherous. Some rentals are in remote areas on the outskirts of town rather than right off main roads. Make sure you understand cancellation and pet policies.

Townsend (population 500) is 18
miles from Pigeon Forge. It is not
built up like neighboring cities so
there is less traffic and noise and
crowds. Highlights: Tuckaleechee
Caverns, Smoky Mountains River Rat
Tubing, Little River Railroad &
Lumber Company Museum, Lily Barn
Garden, Dark Island Swinging
Bridge, and Great Smoky Mountains
Heritage Center. Dancing Bear Lodge
and Tuckaleechee Retreat Center &
Cabins offer best lodging options.
Dining: Riverstone Restaurant,
Trailhead Steak & Trout, Dancing
Bear Appalachian Bistro, and Apple
Valley Café.

NORTH CAROLINA GATEWAY CITIES

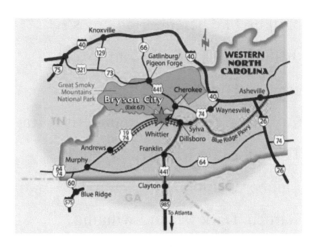

On the North Carolina side, **Bryson City** is the closest gateway city to the park. This small town (population 2,000) is a good stop. Its downtown is filled with quaint shops and restaurants, and the Great Smoky

Mountain Train Depot is right in the heart of it.

One thing you have to do is hop aboard the **Great Smoky Mountains Railroad.** Choose from different scenic routes to see the Nantahala Gorge, Fontana Lake, Tuckasegee River, and more. The train is particularly popular during fall colors and weekends, so be sure to plan ahead if interested. www.gsmr.com

Smoky Mountain Trains Museum is impressive with its collection of thousands of Lionel™ engines, cars, accessories and track design/layout ,

plus a children's activity center and
large gift shop. $. Admission is free if
you purchase any ticket on the Great
Smoky Mountains Railroad.
https://www.gsmr.com/smoky-
mountain-trains-museum/

**Deep Creek Tube Center &
Campground** rents tubes you can
take inside the national park. Follow
the signs to the river put-in to go
tubing. There is a one-mile section of
the Deep River that is designated for
tubing with one part being a "lazy
river" experience and the other part
being a "whitewater" experience.
Some say this is the best tubing in the

Smokies. The campground rents both rustic and modern cabins and has campsites for tents and RVs. There is a Gem Mine on site, free Wi-Fi, and a camp store.

www.deepcreekcamping.com

FYI: Bryson City, NC is 13 miles from the NC side of the park.

Deep Creek Trail is a five-mile trail that is just five minutes from downtown Bryson City. It is very popular because it is scenic and considered an easy walk. No pets.
https://www.greatsmokies.com/wp-content/uploads/2018/05/DeepCreekTrails.pdf

Swain County Heritage Museum, housed in the courthouse, shares the history and heritage of Swain County through photos, films, artifacts, and activities. FREE.

Cooper Creek Trout Farm & Pond is 70 acres of small streams, springs, waterfalls and ponds. Trout fishing is allowed year-round. No reservations required. http://www.cooperscreektroutpond.com/

Deep Creek Winery has outdoor seating so you can enjoy the fabulous mountain view while enjoying a glass of wine and a charcuterie platter (includes fresh Amish cheese).

www.deepcreekwinery.com

**Fly Fishing Museum of the
Southern Appalachians** uses short
films and exhibits, to reveal the
history of fly fishing rods and reels,
gear, and game fishing in this part of
the country. The building is a
dismantled tobacco barn from Surry
County that was reconstructed into a
museum. www.flyfishingmuseum.org

The Tunnel to Nowhere (also known as The Road to Nowhere) was supposed to be a new road but ended up being a road and tunnel to nowhere. Learn the story behind the nowhere road and explore the scenic trails that lay just past the tunnel. You will find the tunnel about ten minutes northwest of Bryson City (six miles inside the park).

More things to do…

Self-guided walking tour (pick up a
map at the visitor's center), Darnell
Fams, Juney Whank Falls Trail,
Wildwater Nantahala Adventure
Center, Tom Branch Falls, Lonesome
Pine Overlook, Indian Creek Falls,
and Nantahala Gorge Canopy Tours,
Nantahala Kid Zip (ziplining), and
Appalachian Rivers Aquarium.

Dining & Drinking: Nantahala Brewing Company, Unplugged Pub, Mountain Layers Brewing Company, Mountain Coffee, Mickey's Pub, Jimmy Mac's Restaurant, Soda Pop's, The Chocolate Shoppe, CJ's Grille, Derailed of Bryson City, The Bistro (Everett Hotel), Everett Street Diner, High Test Deli, Fuller's Farmhouse Kitchen, and Pasqualino's Italian Restaurant.

Accommodations: River's Edge Motel, Stonebrook Lodge, McKinley Edwards Inn, Nantahala Village, Everett Hotel, Microtel Inn & Suites by Wyndham, Nantahala Cabins,

Ridgetop Motel & Campground, and
Hemlock Inn. Also, there are private
rentals available through local
booking companies and large
agencies, such as Booking.com and
Expedia.com.

Looking for something special?
Skyridge Yurts lets you pick the
style yurt you want!
https://www.skyridgeyurts.com/ and
Gorgeous Stays offers a unique
selection of tiny houses, a Skoolie,
deluxe British Double-Decker Bus,
and comfy Glamping Tents.
https://www.gorgeousstays.com/

Cherokee, NC

Oconaluftee Indian Village is a living history museum, recreated from 1760. Learn history, interact with the villagers as they weave baskets, fashion beadworks, make masks, hull canoes, and more. See blowgun demonstrations. Watch warfare preparations and more.

Museum of the Cherokee Indian is a state-of-the-art facility. Through unique displays, interactive video, and a full sensory experience, you will learn 12,000 years of history.

Unto These Hills is an outdoor drama that shares the story of these Cherokee Indians. It is one of the longest running and best outdoor dramas in America. I was impressed with everything from lighting to fighting.

Harrah's Cherokee Casino Resort is a 21-story, four-star luxury hotel with deluxe rooms and spacious suites

with full amenities. There is a huge
conference center, pools, multiple
restaurants, shopping, arcade,
bowling, shows, gaming stations, and
the Mandara Spa, a 15,000-square
foot luxurious spa with a complete
collection of face and body
treatments. The highlight, of course,
is the 150,000-square-foot casino with
3,000 slot machines and 160 table
games, as well as a casino bar.
https://www.caesars.com/harrahs-
cherokee

**FYI: Every Friday and Saturday
night during the summer there is a
Cherokee Bonfire where you can
hear stories and legends that have
been passed down generation to
generation from some of the
greatest storytellers in Cherokee**

Qualla Arts & Crafts Mutual, Inc.
is the oldest Native American co-op
in America. Visitors will be amazed at
the 350 juried artisans creating
traditional Cherokee pottery, jewelry,
baskets, masks, and more.

**To make reservations or buy tickets
for anything in Cherokee,
www.visitcherokeenc.com.**

Sequoyah National Golf Club is owned by the Eastern Band of the Cherokee, this Robert Trent Jones II design is open to the public and offers golfers panoramic vistas on every hole.

https://www.sequoyahnational.com/

FYI: Cherokee is 3 miles from the NC side of the park.

Fire Mountain Trails are 10.5 miles of hiking and biking trails. The parking lot and trailhead is 100 yards from the Oconaluftee Indian Village.

Fishing. Obtain a fishing permit at any of the 28 fishing license locations

throughout Cherokee or at
www.fishcherokee.com.

There are cabins, cottages,
campgrounds, motels, and hotels in
the area.
https://visitcherokeenc.com/stay/cabin
s-and-campgrounds/

Maggie Valley is 17 miles from the
Great Smoky Mountains National
Park's Cataloochee Valley. There is
not much here except **Cataloochee
Valley** and Cataloochee Ski Area.
Maggie Valley Ghost Town in the
Sky is permanently closed.

GREAT SMOKY MOUNTAINS NATIONAL PARK FAST FACTS

County: Swain & Haywood counties in North Carolina; Sevier, Blount, & Cocke counties in Tennessee

Size: Great Smoky Mountains National Park covers 522,427 acres, divided almost evenly between the states of North Carolina and Tennessee. Great Smoky Mountains National Park is situated on over 800 square miles of the Southern Appalachians between Tennessee and North Carolina.

Appalachian Trail: The Smokies offer the best part of the Appalachian Trail. Of the 2,147 miles that comprise the trail, the Great Smoky Mountains National Park accounts for 71 miles, including the highest peak along the entire trail (Clingmans Dome 6,643').

FYI: *The difference between the Blue Ridge Mountains and the Smoky Mountains...*

The Great Smoky Mountains are a subrange of the Blue Ridge Mountain System. Thus, the Great Smokies are the Blue Ridge Mountains, but not all of the Blue Ridge Mountains are Great Smoky Mountains. The Blue Ridge Mountains stretch 615 miles from Carlisle, Pennsylvania southwestward into Mount Oglethorpe, Georgia.

Nearest Parks: The closest national parks are Mammoth Cave and Congaree. Both are roughly 4 hours away.

175

Nearest Cities: Cherokee, Maggie Valley, and Bryson City (North Carolina) and Gatlinburg, Pigeon Forge, Sevierville (Tennessee).

Time Zone: Eastern Standard Time

Average Temperatures: The warm season lasts for 4.0 months, from May 23 to September 22, with an average daily high temperature above 77°F. The hottest month of the year in Great Smoky Mountains National Park is July, with an average high of 84°F and low of 65°F.

The cold season lasts for 2.9 months, from December 1 to February 27, with an average daily high temperature below 54°F. The coldest month of the year in Great Smoky Mountains National Park is January,

with an average low of 29°F and high
of 47°F.

FYI: The Smokies are twice as big as The Rockies.

Language: English but Appalachian
English is American English native to the
Appalachian mountain region of the
Eastern United States. Historically, the
term "Appalachian dialect" refers to a local
English variety of southern Appalachia

Currency: American Dollar (USD).
In addition to cash, credit and debit
cards are also widely received.
Cashless alternatives (like Apple Pay)
are available in some places but not
widely accepted in the park or some
of the smaller communities nearby.

Nickname: *"The Smokies."* If you've been before or when you go, you will notice a "smokiness" about the mountains. That is because there is a blue-colored fog or smoky-like appearance here. It is not caused by solely by pollution like some think but rather mostly by plants within the park. The leaves, roots, and flowers of trees and plants give off volatile organic compound (VOC). Wherever there are VOCs, there is a vapor that creates a fog or smokiness. Since the

park is comprised of millions of
plants, the mountains always appear
smoky or foggy. Natural VOCs are
harmless. Long-term exposure to the
VOCs created by pollution are a
different story.

Check out this short film
highlighting the best of the park:
https://morethanjustparks.com/great
-smoky-mountains-national-park-
facts/ (*Warning!*
It will make you want to go the park
ASAP!)

TERRANCE'S TOP TEN PICKS

1.   Go spelunking In

Tuckaleechee Caverns

Tuckaleechee Caverns is a mile-long
limestone cave system full of
enormous stalagmites, streams, and
Silver Falls, a 210-foot underground
waterfall. It is the tallest subterranean
waterfall in the eastern United States.

Tuckaleechee Caverns is rated the #1
cave (most popular) in the eastern
U.S. and has been awarded the
prestigious AAA Exclusive Five Star
Gem Attraction.

Tuckaleechee Caverns is also home to
the most sensitive seismic station on
Earth. These caves became home to a
seismic station when the Tennessee

Valley Authority was building dams in the area and wanted to know the impact of the water on the underlying tectonic plates.

Because of the caverns' deep, solid, limestone formations, the caves can pick up on sounds on the other side of the globe. The US military now uses this seismic station to monitor nuclear testing around the world. Currently, the Tuckaleechee Caverns AS107 seismic station is monitored 24/7 and transmits via satellite to the Department of Defense, US Military, Geneva Switzerland, Vienna Austria, the Comprehensive Nuclear Test Ban

Treaty Organization (CTBTO), and the Pentagon. It is has been able to detect nuclear testing in North Korea, as well as monitor earthquakes across the globe. *Amazing!*

Spelunking is a fancy word for "exploring caves as you walk/climb/squeeze and crawl through tight passages." Normally, visitors to this cave take a guided one-mile walk that includes a stop in the "Big Room," which is so big it is nearly the size of a football stadium. Spelunking takes you into areas of the cave that are normally off limits and more challenging to explore.

Carved inside the earth's oldest

mountain chain, Tuckaleechee is

estimated to be twenty to thirty

million years old.

825 Cavern Road, Townsend

https://tuckaleecheecaverns.com/

FYI: Tennessee has the largest number of caves in the U.S., at least 10,000! There is even another cave system nearby, Forbidden Caverns, 455 Blowing Cave Road, Sevierville, TN

2. Explore a historic "ghost" town.

Elkmont got its start in the mid-1800s as a small settlement of homesteaders, hunters, and loggers. Thanks to a lumber boom, it grew to become the second-largest town in the county with a hotel, store, church, school, and post office.

The Little River Logging Company stopped their operations in this area in 1926. People began leaving and the once thriving town became a ghost town before long.

The park started restoring some of the
remaining buildings and in 1994,
Elkmont was listed on the National
Register of Historic Places.

From Sugarlands Visitors Center,
head west on Fighting Creek Gap
Road (toward Cades Cove). After
about 4.5 miles take a left onto
Elkmont Road.

Troll Bridge

189

FYI: You can also hike the Jakes Creek and Little River trails past stone walls and chimneys, which mark the former locations of cabins that once stood in Elkmont. You'll also see the Elkmont Troll Bridge, another hidden gem in the Smokies. Elkmont Ghost Town is very close to the park's largest campground, Elkmont Campground (https://www.recreation.gov/camping/campgrounds/232487).

**3.   Take a Historic River Town
Ramble.**

Discover a bygone era on a 3-
hour small group tour of Great
Smoky Mountains National
Park. Hear stories about the
Cherokee people and the
settlers who once lived in these
mountains. Find out how these

first families learned how to
survive off the land. During this
historic stroll, you'll visit a
small family cemetery, 19th-
century barn, spring house, and
a small restored cabin. Enjoy
the best of nature and history
during this slow-paced guided
walk through the heart of the
Smokies. Snacks are included.

https://www.viator.com/tours/G
reat-Smoky-Mountains-
National-Park/Explore-a-
Simpler-Time-Smoky-
Mountain-Tour/d24149-
26480P2?mcid=56757

4. Enjoy a Waterfalls & Breweries Tour.

This unique all day tour starts in Bryson City (NC). During this outing, you will visit four gorgeous waterfalls in the Cullasaja River Gorge. On the 2nd and 3rd stop, you will hike down to the falls and back up. In addition to being rewarded with great views of the falls, you wrap up the tour with visits to five breweries. One sample beer at each brewery is included with your tour ticket.

Leave the driving and logistics to someone else. All you have to do is enjoy yourself!
https://www.viator.com/tours/Great-Smoky-Mountains-National-Park/Waterfalls-and-Breweries-Tour/d24149-129200P1

5.   Hike the Appalachian Trail.

(or at least a small part of it). It is said to be a life-changing experience or at the very least, very cathartic. Completed in 1937, this legendary trail stretches some 2,200 uninterrupted miles from the mountains of north Georgia to the

heart of Maine, passing through 14
states in all.

The Appalachian Trail cuts through
the heart of Great Smoky
Mountains National Park and there
are many opportunities to hop on
the legendary trail in the park, even
for a short walk. Clingmans Dome
provides one of the easiest

opportunities to hike a stretch of
the AT. Besides the trail to the
summit, there are several trails that
start from the Clingmans Dome Road
and parking area. The Appalachian
Trail (AT) crosses Clingmans Dome,
marking the highest point along its
journey from Georgia to Maine.
Restrooms and fresh water are
available at Clingman's Dome.

FUN FACTS ABOUT THE
APPALACHIAN TRAIL

- **The Appalachian. Trail is the Longest "Marked Footpath" in America.**
- **Its entire length is about 2,190 miles (3,524.5 km) making it the longest hiking-only trail in the world.**
- **The Smoky Mountains are home to the highest point along the Appalachian Trail.**
- **Only around 500 people hike the entire Appalachian Trail each year as opposed to the 3 million who hike part of the trail each year.**

6.   **You gotta go leaf peeping!**
Check out the fall colors or
whatever you call it. The
Smoky Mountains National
Park has more than 100
native tree species and many of
these trees turn bright orange,
yellow and brilliant shades of
red every fall (usually mid-
September for higher-elevation

colors and mid-October for lower ones). From Sugar Maples to Scarlet Oaks you will be dazzled at Mother Nature. You can drive or hike to see the best nature show around.

Peak leaf season is impossible to predict because it depends on rain, temperature and several other factors. But you can count on the leaves first starting to turn colors in the high elevations where it is cooler. As it gets later in the season, you'll discover leaves changing colors in lower elevations.

If you must plan well in advance, it would most likely be the second half of October for higher-elevation colors, and late-October through the first week of November for lower elevations.

The best places in the park to enjoy this seasonal phenomenon is Clingmans Dome, Look Rock Tower, and Mount Le Conte.

Be warned that this is the busiest time of year in the park. There will be crowds and traffic, so be prepared.

FYI: Ssshh! Top secret but if you want to avoid the traffic and crowds, (1) take the Blue Ridge Parkway north of Cherokee, N.C., on US 441. Or (2) take the Roaring Fork Motor Nature Trail. From downtown Gatlinburg, turn the 8th stoplight onto Historic Nature Trail/Airport Road. Follow it into the park and travel on Roaring Fork Nature Trail. There are pull offs on route for viewing and photo ops.

**Check out the Gatlinburg
Fall Colors
Forecast**
www.gatlinburgtnguide.com/fall-
colors-forecast/

7.   **Cross the longest pedestrian
suspension bridge in North
America.** *Can you say photo
op!*

The bridge is 680 feet across
a valley situated 140 feet
below and 500 feet above
Gatlinburg. It is 1800 feet
above sea level. There is a

glass bottom at the highest point so you can see for yourselves—if you dare!

To get to the bridge, you enjoy a chair lift to the top of SkyLift. Check out the views of Gatlinburg from the top of Crockett Mountain.

**FYI: The SkyLift is one of the
oldest continuously operated
attractions in the Smoky
Mountains.
https://www.gatlinburgskylift
.com/tickets**

8.   **Enjoy an epic road trip!**
The famed Blue Ridge
Parkway begins in the Great
Smoky Mountains National
Park. This is one of the best
scenic drives on the East
Coast. You can journey from
the Great Smoky Mountains
National Park all the way up
to Shenandoah National Park
in Virginia. Stop for a picnic
lunch, a hike, and/or roadside
attractions along the way. It

is 338 miles so you should allow a couple of days so you can fully enjoy the experience. Route highlights include: Linville Falls, Asheville, Blue Ridge Music Center, Mabry Mill and Craggy Gardens. https://www.blueridgeparkway.org/ and https://www.nps.gov/shen/index.htm

9.   **You have to go on a hike!** You
can't visit one of the best
national parks in our country
and not go on a hike. I
recommend the Gatlinburg
Trail because it is considered
easy (3.8 mile roundtrip) on
level terrain. It is also very
scenic. Furthermore, it is dog
friendly if your dog is in good
shape and accustomed to long
walks (make sure you have

water for him). It is a stroller
friendly trail too. Also, you
don't have to do the whole trail.
You can turn around at any
time if you so choose. It is two
miles to the Sugarlands Visitors
Center so you can relax and
enjoy some refreshments and
use the facilities before turning
around or going on.

The hike is along the west
prong of the Little Pigeon River
and cross a footbridge, enjoying
mountain views and ruins of
historic homesteads along the
way.

916 River Road, Gatlinburg

https://www.nps.gov/grsm/planyour
visit/gatlinburg-trail.htm

**FYI: Children ages 5 – 12 can
become Junior Rangers. Get a
Junior Ranger Booklet ($) online or
at any visitor's center. There are
different books to choose from.
Complete the fun assignments and
turn it in to any ranger who will
give you a junior ranger badge!**

10. Take a thrilling Rail Ride & then go Ziplining. Children must be at least ten years old. The two-hour scenic train trip starts in Bryson City at the Great Smoky

Mountain Railroad
depot. Travel through the
heart of the Smokies,
along Fontana Lake, and
up into Nantahala Gorge.
You will disembark the
train at the Wildwater
Nantahala Gorge Canopy
Tours station. There are
thirteen different ziplines
and eight skybridges! All
transportation is
included. You will return
to Bryson City where
your adventure began.
Anyone in the group who
can't or don't want to go

ziplining have the option
to stay on the train
roundtrip.

You can choose the **Raft &
Rail** adventure if whitewater
rafting is more your thing.
https://www.gsmr.com/packages/

About The Great Smoky Mountains National Park

The Great Smoky Mountains are among the oldest mountains in the world, dating back millions of years.

But it wasn't until 1926 that they became the Great Smoky Mountains National Park.

President Calvin Coolidge signed a bill that established the Great Smoky Mountain National Park to protect the land and wildlife. The Park would include land from two states: Tennessee and North Carolina.

John D. Rockefeller, Jr., the son of oil tycoon, John D. Rockefeller, made a significant contribution to the park.

In 1928, he gave $5 million (that's $86 million and some change in today's dollars) from his family's foundation, to help acquire land for the park.

This contribution was critical because most of the area needed to create the park was owned by lumber companies.

His financial support helped to buy the land and made it easier to negotiate with the lumber companies.

In 1934, North Carolina and Tennessee donated 300,000 acres of land for the park. This was prudent because the establishment of a national park kept the state from losing all of its most important forest to the lumber companies. The park not only saved the land and its inhabitants, but outlying communities grew and flourished as a result.

A survey commissioned by the National Park Service showed that visitors to the GSMNP spent more

than $818 million in gateway
communities located around the
boundaries of the national park.

Visitors to national parks and other
nearby federal lands contribute
billions to regional economies
while creating hundreds of
thousands of private sector jobs.
This has a domino effect on
communities near those
communities and state-wide.
Ultimately, benefiting the entire
U.S. population as a nation.

Another 150,000 acres had to be
bought from the people who lived
there. Money to buy the land was

raised by state legislatures and citizens (even school children). Remarkably, $10 million was raised.

In the 1930s, the Civilian Conservation Corp (CCC) worked to get the park ready for visitors. They built roads, bridges, hiking trails, and campgrounds for people to enjoy. In September of 1940, the park was officially opened by President Franklin Delano Roosevelt at Newfound Gap.

FYI: By the time the CCC was terminated in 1942, a total of 2 million had performed work in 198 CCC camps in 94 national park and monument areas and 697 camps in 881 state, county and municipal areas. Through the CCC program 711 state parks had been established. Overall, the CCC planted more than three billion trees and constructed trails and shelters in more than 800 parks nationwide during its nine years of existence. It helped to shape the modern national and state park systems we enjoy today.

Today, the Great Smoky Mountain
National Park is well over 500,000
acres between Tennessee and North
Carolina. The Great Smoky
Mountains National Park is the most
biodiverse park in America! More
than 19,000 species have been
documented in the park, and scientists
believe an additional 80,000-100,000
may live there! There are more than
1,600 species of flowering plants,
including 100 native tree species and
more than 100 native shrub species.
There are also about 65 species of
mammals, more than 200 varieties of
birds, 67 native fish species and more
than 80 types of reptiles and

amphibians! Additionally, there are roughly 100 historic buildings within the park.

The Cherokee people were the first to call the Smokies home. The Cherokee considered the mountains to be a sacred place and referred to the area as "Shaconage" (Sha-Kon-O-Hey): land of the blue smoke. They hunted, fished, and farmed the land until conflict arose with arriving white settlers that ended with them surrendering their land.

In 1838, 14,000 Cherokee of the Cherokee Nation began their journey west on the Trail of Tears. But

another group of Cherokee, the
Oconaluftee Cherokee, were allowed
to stay. These Cherokee had an
advisor, William H. Thomas, who
helped them with legal matters.

The Oconaluftee Cherokee, along
with some members of the Cherokee
Nation who hid in the mountains to
avoid relocation, became the Eastern
Band of the Cherokees.

Today, there are about 11,000
members who mostly live within the
reservation in western North Carolina.
The reservation is a big part of the
local economy.

Five Fun Facts about the Park

Spotted Salamander

1. It is the **Salamander Capital of the World**. Thirty different species of salamanders (also known as spring lizards) call the park home. The Smoky Mountain Hellbenders are the largest aquatic and are the rarest in the park. Salamanders have absorbent skin and the

225

oils, salts and lotions on
our hands can do serious
damage.

2. The Smokies have 2,900
miles of streams—and all
of them allow fishing! In
fact, most streams are at
or close to their carrying
capacity of fish.

3. Higher elevations rarely
go above 80∘F.

4. The Great Smoky
Mountains National Park
is one of the only
national parks that does
not charge an admission
fee and is open 24/7.

5. An average weekend
welcomes 60,000 visitors
to the park. This
excludes fall colors,
summer, and holidays

when the numbers are
probably closer to 80,000
- 100,000.

**FYI: There is no access fee charged
for any TN state park. All 57 state
parks in Tennessee are free to enter
and enjoy. However, some park
activities may require permits or
reservations. The five state parks
closest to the Great Smoky
Mountains National Park are Seven
Islands State Birding Park, Fort
Loudoun, Big Ridge State Park,
Panther Creek State Park, and
Warrior's Path State Park.**

Smokies Talk

- Kindly —In Appalachian English, it means *kind of*. For example, Matt *kindly* likes Alice.

- Story — If someone states that you're telling a *story*, they think you're lying.
- Reach Me — This is used when someone is asking you to hand them something.
- Fixin' — In conversational use, *fixin'* means that you're preparing to or heading out to go do something — "I'm *fixin'* to go into town this afternoon."
- Cumfluttered — If you're confused or embarrassed, this is the perfect Appalachian adjective.

- Chancy — A good word to use when you're feeling doubtful about a situation.
- Do wha? — This one is self-explanatory — "You want me to *do wha*!?"

FYI: The 500-foot Fontana Dam (located in the SE corner of the park) is the tallest concrete dam east of the Mississippi River. It helps provide electricity for residents of the Tennessee Valley.

Popular Appalachian Phrases

- Cut a shine — You can ask someone to *cut a shine* if you want them to dance with you.
- Eh, law — This basically means "Oh, well."
- From can see to can't see — This Smokies phrase is a fun way to say "from dawn to dusk."
- Pay it no mind — This means something akin to "don't let it bother you."
- Beginning to turn — This is used when someone is nearing the end of their life.
- Zonies alive! — A bit of a swear often used to express

shock, excitement, or surprise; something akin to "Holy sh*t!"

- Redd up — This phrase is often used when people are getting their homes ready for visitors by cleaning and organizing.
- Lay out — If you fake being sick to get out of a responsibility, then you're *laying out*!
- Fair up — This phrase is used if the weather was poor and then *fairs up* for the better.
- A pig in a poke — This phrase is used when you're buying something without knowing everything about it, implying that there's something unwanted you don't yet know about.

FYI: Most people think that Dolly Parton's childhood home was in Pigeon Forge because that is where Dollywood is located. However, Parton's childhood home was a tiny cabin in Locust Ridge, eleven miles away from Pigeon Forge. However, Dolly's brother built a replica in Dollywood of the cabin and her mother decorated the interior with reproductions to best represent how the home really was. Dollywood visitors can see it as part of their admission price.

ANNUAL EVENTS & AVERAGE TEMPS

It rains *a lot* in the Smokies, especially at higher elevations. It rains more on the higher peaks (as much as 85 inches) than anywhere else in the country except the Pacific Northwest. Some of the upper elevation areas are classified as temperate rainforests.

For details about these events and to find a complete list of annual events, https://www.visitmysmokies.com/what-to-do/smoky-mountain-events/

FYI: There are probably more car shows in this area than anywhere else in America. If you are a car enthusiast, there are events every single month!

233

January

New Year celebrations (various locations)

Winter Heritage Festival

February

Winterfest

Wilderness Wildlife Week

Smoky Mountain Gospel Jubilee

March

Hands On Gatlinburg

St. Patrick's Celebrations

Launch of Rafting Season

April

Spring Smoky Mountain Trout Tournament

Great Smoky Easter Arts & Crafts Show

Spring Rod Run (car show)

Dollywood's Flower & Food Festival

Spring Wildflower Pilgrimage

May

Scottish Festival & Games

Bloomin' BBQ & Bluegrass Festival

Slammedenuff Car Show

Firefly Light Show (Mother Nature puts on this widely popular show in late May every year. Tickets are required and are obtained for lottery service from the National Park Service).

<u>June</u>

Smallmouth King Bass Fishing Tournament

A Mountain Quiltfest

Tumbler Invasion Craft Show

Summer in the Smokies

Dollywood Summer Celebration

 **<u>July</u>**

Gatlinburg First Independence Day
Parade in the Nation

Gatlinburg River Raft Regatta

Gatlinburg Fireworks Finale

Patriot Festival

Gatlinburg's Summer Craftsmen's
Fair

Summer in the Smokies

Dollywood Summer Celebration

August

Harvest Fest at Rocky Top Wine Fest

Summer in the Smokies

Dollywood Summer Celebration

September

Fall Rod Run (car show)

Dumplin Valley Bluegrass Festival

Smoky Mountain Truck Fest

Dollywood Harvest Festival

Pigeon Forge Bluegrass Festival

 **October**

Great Pumpkin LumiNights at
Dollywood

Sevierville's Smoky Mountain
Harvest Festival

National Quartet Convention

Gatlinburg's Fall Craftsmen's Festival

History & Haunts

Pigeon Forge Halloween Spooktacular

Holiday Shopping Expo

November

Dollywood's Smoky Mountain Christmas

Ice Skating at Wilderness at the Smokies

Shadrack's Christmas Wonderland

Winterfest Trolley Ride of Lights

Gatlinburg Winter Magic & Chili Cookoff

December

Dollywood's Smoky Mountain Christmas

Shadrack's Christmas Wonderland

Winterfest Trolley Ride of Lights

Ice Skating at Wilderness at the Smokies

Gatlinburg's Festival of Lights Parade includes dancers, marching bands, musicians, and Santa, of course.

Winterfest Driving Tour of Lights on Pigeon Forge Parkway takes place from November to February. Pink Jeep Tours and the Redneck Comedy Bus Tour will drive you around to

enjoy the millions of lights and
displays if you prefer not to drive.

Polar Express Train Ride (offered
by Great Smoky Mountains Railroad
in Bryson City) takes visitors on a
magical ride to the North Pole with
Santa stopping in along the way.
Enjoy decorations, cocoa and
storytelling.

**Titanic Museum Christmas &
Winter Celebration** takes place early
November to early January. There are
Christmas lights and decorations
everywhere.

Average Temps in the Park

Month	High / Low (°F)
January	41° / 18°
February	45° / 21°
March	54° / 27°
April	63° / 34°
May	69° / 43°
June	75° / 51°
July	78° / 55°
August	77° / 54°
September	72° / 48°
October	63° / 36°
November	53° / 27°
December	44° / 21 F

How to Pack

This really depends on how much
outdoors stuff you'll be doing and the
time of year you visit. If you plan to
explore the park and be on foot a
good bit, you will need:

*good hiking boots (sneakers are okay
around town but not so much in the
park where thicker, better soles are
needed for rough terrain and long
hikes

*good walking socks (don't skimp on
cost-buy quality; your feet will thank
you)

*good rain jacket (always bring it
with you even when it doesn't look
like rain or not being forecast to rain;
you will thank me later!)

*drinks and snacks (always carry bottled water and trail snacks at the very least)

FYI: There are no restaurants inside the Great Smoky Mountains Park, so you'll need to bring a sack lunch for a day trip or food for meals while camping. The Cades Cove Campground Store does has a limited variety of groceries. The store also has grab-and-go breakfast items, hot and cold sandwiches, pizza and soft-serve ice cream.

*essential medications like an EpiPen or diabetic injections and others like allergy medication (keep 24hr supply on you or in the car for those days when you will be out for hours)

*first aid kit

*compass (optional)

*bear spray (should not be used
unless the bear shows signs of
aggression)

*pet supplies (if bringing your pet
along these should include a sealable
bowl for fresh water at all times, food,
bed, leash, ID tag, favorite toy, and
dog treats)

**FYI: Always dress in layers you can
remove and add as temperatures
change through the day and night. I
have 2-in-1 pants that zip off to
become shorts or stay pants. They
are essential for travel! Wear
breathable athletic clothing that is
not too tight (comfy is more
important than appearance!)**

*shorts (if going during summer months)

*All weather coat, gloves, scarf, hat (if going during winter months)

*sandals/flip flops/beach shoes

*walking shoes

*gear (fishing rod, scuba mask, surfboard, floats, pool noodles, boogie boards, etc.)

*bathing suit(s) and cover up

*t-shirts

*lightweight pants

*resort casual 'dress' clothes (if planning to dine at upscale restaurant)

*30 SPF sunscreen and hat
(sunglasses optional)

*insect repellent

*light sweater (if you are cold-natured
you may want one in places where the
A/C is working well)

*waterproof fanny pack or waterproof
backpack (to safeguard phone,
camera, wallet, etc.)

*toiletries and cosmetics (be sure to
pack these items in a zippered bag or
at least put liquid items in a Ziploc
bag so that there are no spills or leaks
on your clothes or electronics)

*medications (make sure you have
enough for three days longer than
your trip, just in case you are delayed
for any reason)

*documents (including a park map)

*flashlight or headlamp

*disposable paper or plastic bags for trash (please remove whatever you use!)

*extra batteries, sim cards, flash drives, cords and/or chargers

*entertainment (device loaded with games, eBooks, and shows/movies or bring books, playing cards, DVDs, and old-fashioned board games.

 **FYI: Take pictures on your phone of all tickets and confirmations, just in case you lose the originals.**

TERRANCE ZEPKE
Series Reading Order & Guide

Series List

Most Haunted Series
Terrance Talks Travel Series
Cheap Travel Series
Spookiest Series
Strange Series
Weird & Wonderful Travels
Stop Talking Series
Carolinas for Kids Series Ghosts of the Carolinas Series
Books & Guides for the Carolinas Series
& More Books by Terrance Zepke

≈

Introduction

Here is a list of titles by Terrance Zepke. They are presented in chronological order although they do not need to bc read in any particular order.

Also included is an author bio, a personal message from Terrance, and some other information you may find helpful.

Most books are available in digital and print formats. They can be found on all major booksellers or ordered through your favorite independent bookseller.

For more about this author and her books visit her Author Page at:
http://www.amazon.com/Terrance-Zepke/e/B000APJNIA/.

You can also connect with Terrance on Twitter @terrancezepke or on

www.facebook.com/terrancezepke
www.pinterest.com/terrancezepke
www.goodreads.com/terrancezepke

Sign up for weekly email notifications of the **Terrance Talks Travel** blog and receive a FREE 50-page CHEAP TRAVEL REPORT and be the first to learn about new episodes of Uber Adventures, cheap travel tips & resources, and her TRIP PICK OF THE WEEK at www.terrancetalkstravel.com or sign up for her **Mostly Ghostly** blog at www.terrancezepke.com.

≈

You can follow her travel show, **TERRANCE TALKS TRAVEL: ÜBER ADVENTURES on** www.blogtalkradio.com/terrancetalkstravel or subscribe to it on **iTunes.**

Warning: Listening to this show could lead to a spectacular South African safari, hot-air ballooning over the Swiss Alps, Disney Adventures, and Tornado Tours!

AUTHOR BIO

Terrance Zepke studied Journalism at the University of Tennessee and later received a Master's degree in Mass Communications from the University of South Carolina. And she studied parapsychology at the renowned Rhine Research Center.

Zepke spends much of her time happily traveling around the world but always returns home to the Carolinas where she lives part-time in both states. She has written hundreds of articles and more than fifty books. She is also the host of *Terrance Talks Travel: Über Adventures.* Additionally, this award-winning and best-selling author has been featured in many publications and programs, such as NPR, CNN, *The Washington Post*, *Adventure Journal*, Associated Press, Travel with Rick Steves, Around the World, *Publishers Weekly*, *Woman's*

Day, World Travel & Dining with Pierre Wolfe, Good Morning Show, The Learning Channel, and The Travel Channel.

When she's not investigating haunted places, searching for pirate treasure, or climbing lighthouses, she is most likely packing for her next adventure to some far flung place, such as Reykjavik or Kwazulu Natal. Some of her favorite adventures include piranha fishing on the Amazon, shark cage diving in South Africa, hiking the Andes Mountains Inca Trail, camping in the Himalayas, dog-sledding in the Arctic Circle, and a gorilla safari in the Congo.

≈

MOST HAUNTED SERIES

A Ghost Hunter's Guide to the Most Haunted Places in America

A Ghost Hunter's Guide to the Most Haunted Houses in America

A Ghost Hunter's Guide to the Most Haunted Hotels & Inns in America

A Ghost Hunter's Guide to the Most Haunted Historic Sites in America

A Ghost Hunter's Guide to the Most Haunted Places in the World

The Ghost Hunter's MOST HAUNTED Box Set (3 in 1): Discover America's Most Haunted Destinations

MOST HAUNTED and SPOOKIEST Sampler Box Set: Featuring *A GHOST HUNTER'S GUIDE TO THE MOST HAUNTED PLACES IN AMERICA* and *SPOOKIEST CEMETERIES*

The Quirky Tourist Guide to The Great Smoky Mountains National Park | Terrance Zepke

TERRANCE TALKS TRAVEL SERIES

Terrance Talks Travel: A Pocket Guide to South Africa

Terrance Talks Travel: A Pocket Guide to African Safaris

Terrance Talks Travel: A Pocket Guide to Adventure Travel

Terrance Talks Travel: A Pocket Guide to Florida Keys (including Key West & The Everglades)

Terrance Talks Travel: The Quirky Tourist Guide to Key West

Terrance Talks Travel: The Quirky Tourist Guide to Cape Town

Terrance Talks Travel: The Quirky Tourist Guide to Reykjavik (Iceland)

Terrance Talks Travel: The Quirky Tourist Guide to Charleston, South Carolina

Terrance Talks Travel: The Quirky Tourist Guide to Ushuaia (The Gateway to Antarctica)

The Quirky Tourist Guide to The Great
Smoky Mountains National Park | Terrance
Zepke

*Terrance Talks Travel: The Quirky Tourist
Guide to Antarctica*

*Terrance Talks Travel: The Quirky Tourist
Guide to Machu Picchu & Cuzco (Peru)*

*Terrance Talks Travel: A Pocket Guide to
East Africa's Uganda and Rwanda*

*Terrance Talks Travel: The Quirky
Tourist Guide to Kathmandu (Nepal) & The
Himalayas*

*Terrance Talks Travel: The Quirky
Tourist Guide to Edinburgh, Scotland*

*Terrance Talks Travel: The Quirky
Tourist Guide to Marrakesh, Morocco*

*Terrance Talks Travel: The Quirky
Tourist Guide to Myrtle Beach, South
Carolina*

*Terrance Talks Travel: The Quirky Tourist
Guide to Savannah, Georgia*

The Quirky Tourist Guide to The Great
Smoky Mountains National Park | Terrance
Zepke

*Terrance Talks Travel: A Pocket Guide to
New Zealand*

*Terrance Talks Travel: The Quirky Tourist
Guide to Queensland, Australia*

*Terrance Talks Travel: The Quirky Tourist
Guide to Sydney, Australia*

*Terrance Talks Travel: The Quirky Tourist
Guide to Lapland (Arctic Circle) &
Helsinki, Finland*

Terrance Talks Travel: Cheap London

Terrance Talks Travel: Cheap Disney

*Terrance Talks Travel: The Quirky
Tourist Guide to Amsterdam*

*Terrance Talks Travel: Cheap Las
Vegas*

*Terrance Talks Travel: The Quirky Tourist
Guide to the Outer Banks, North Carolina*

*Terrance Talks Travel: The Quirky Tourist
Guide to Wilmington & the Cape Fear
Coast, North Carolina*

259

The Quirky Tourist Guide to The Great Smoky Mountains National Park | Terrance Zepke

Terrance Talks Travel: A Guide to Living Abroad for Digital Nomads & Expats

Terrance Talks Travel: The Quirky Tourist Guide to the Great Smoky Mountains National Park

Terrance Talks Travel: The Quirky Tourist Guide to Costa Rica

Terrance Talks Travel: The Quirky Tourist Guide to Virginia's Historic Triangle (Williamsburg, Jamestown & Yorktown)

African Safari Box Set: Featuring TERRANCE TALKS TRAVEL: *A Pocket Guide to South Africa* and *TERRANCE TALKS TRAVEL: A Pocket Guide to African Safaris*

≈

CHEAP TRAVEL SERIES

How to Cruise Cheap!

How to Fly Cheap!

How to Travel Cheap!

How to Travel FREE or Get Paid to Travel!

CHEAP TRAVEL SERIES (4 IN 1) BOX SET (2017)

SPOOKIEST SERIES

Spookiest Lighthouses

Spookiest Battlefields

Spookiest Cemeteries

Spookiest Objects

Spookiest Military Bases, Ships, Museums,
& Forts

Spookiest Box Set (3 in 1): Discover
America's Most Haunted Destinations
(Spookiest Lighthouses, Spookiest
Battlefields & Spookiest Cemeteries)

MOST HAUNTED and SPOOKIEST
Sampler Box Set: Featuring *A GHOST*
HUNTER'S GUIDE TO THE MOST
HAUNTED PLACES IN AMERICA and
SPOOKIEST CEMETERIES

≈

WEIRD & WONDERFUL TRAVEL SERIES

The World's Weirdest Museums

The World's Weirdest Attractions

The World's Weirdest Accommodations
(Coming Soon!)

STRANGE SERIES

The Most Cursed Places in the World

The Creepiest Places in the World

≈

STOP TALKING SERIES

Stop Talking & Start Writing Your Book

Stop Talking & Start Publishing Your Book

Stop Talking & Start Selling Your Book

Stop Talking & Start Writing Your Book Series (3 in 1) Box Set (Writing, Publishing & Selling Your Book)

MORE BOOKS

Lighthouses of the Carolinas for Kids
Pirates of the Carolinas for Kids
Ghosts of the Carolinas for Kids
Ghosts of the Carolina Coasts
The Best Ghost Tales of South Carolina
Ghosts & Legends of the Carolina Coasts
The Best Ghost Tales of North Carolina
Pirates of the Carolinas
Lighthouses of the Carolinas: A Short History & Guide
Lowcountry Voodoo: Tales, Spells & Boo Hags
Happy Halloween! Hundreds of Perfect Party Recipes, Delightful Decorating Ideas & Awesome Activities
Ghosts of Savannah
How to Train Your Puppy or Dog Using Three Simple Strategies (FUN & FAST!)
*Fiction books are written under a pseudonym.

Message from the Author

The primary purpose of this guide is to introduce you to some titles you may not have known about. Another reason for it is to let you know all the ways you can connect with me. Authors love to hear from readers. We truly appreciate you more than you'll ever know. Please feel free to send me a comment or question via the comment form found on every page on www.terrancezepke.com and www.terrancetalkstravel.com or follow me on your favorite social media. Don't forget that you can also listen to my travel show, **Terrance Talks Travel: Über Adventures** on Blog Talk Radio, Amazon Podcasts, and iTunes. The best way to make sure you don't miss any episodes of these shows (and find a complete archive of shows), new book releases and giveaways, cheap travel tips, free downloadable travel reports, and more is to subscribe to *Terrance Talks Travel* on www.terrancetalkstravel.com or *Mostly Ghostly* on www.terrancezepke.com.

Thank you for your interest and HAPPY READING!

Terrance

The Quirky Tourist Guide to The Great Smoky Mountains National Park | Terrance Zepke

See the next page for a sneak peek of the first book in Terrance Zepke's 'weird & wonderful series:

The World's Weirdest Museums

Available from Safari Publishing

Museum of Salt & Pepper Shakers

Location: Gatlinburg, Tennessee

Salt and Pepper Shaker Museum

boasts the world's biggest collection

with more than 22,000 salt and pepper

shaker sets. You can't even imagine all

the designs! *Seriously!* The designs

include the Beatles, Mt. Rushmore,

hundreds of animals and foods, witches,

and much more.

Andrea Ludden and her family

moved to Cosby, Tennessee to open a

museum to exhibit her vast salt and pepper shaker collection. In three short years, Ludden's collection had grown so extensive that the family had to move to bigger digs. They relocated to Gatlinburg, which is a big tourist destination and a quirky mountain community where such a museum would fit right in.

Andrea Ludden is a Belgium, trained archaeologist. As such, she appreciates the history and creativity of each and every one of her shakers. She has lovingly and carefully cultivated the display space to best showcase her exhibits. There is a gift

shop where you can buy a duplicate set

of your favorite shaker set.

This is the question asked most often by
museum visitors:

***Which Shaker has the most amount
of holes - salt or pepper?***

It depends! The number of holes in
salt and pepper shakers varies by
culture, health and taste. Here in the

U.S. excessive salt is considered bad for you, so the salt shaker is the one with the fewer holes, but in parts of Europe it's the other way around. It also has to do with availability – in some places salt was rare and prized, whereas in Europe it was difficult to get your hands on Pepper since it's a spice from the Orient (very exotic) which was used to spice up meat that was past its prime. Another factor is the size of the grains – some salts are quite coarse while others are very fine - and pepper can be ground or it can be cracked, which many cooks prefer. So, what will pour better? Exceptions abound - you can have 1, 2, 3 or more holes in a shaker, and they go from tiny holes to huge ones.

This information was taken from the museum's website.

VISITOR TIPS: Open daily from 10 a.m. – 2 p.m. Children 12 and younger are free. 461 Brookside Village Way (Winery Square) Gatlinburg, Tennessee 37738 (U.S.).
http://thesaltandpeppershakermuseum.com/

 FYI: The small fee charged for adults is applied towards any purchase.

Tea & book shakers—too cute!

Use this link to see more pictures or access a virtual tour of the museum, http://thesaltandpeppershakermuseum.com/Museum-Pictures.

INDEX

H

Made in United States
Troutdale, OR
08/14/2023

12076445R00159